ISAAC ASIMOV'S
Library of the Universe

The SUN

by Isaac Asimov

Gareth Stevens Children's Books
London • Milwaukee

British Library Cataloguing in Publication Data

Asimov, Isaac, 1920-
The sun.
I. Title II. Series
523.7

ISBN 0-83687-014-X

A Gareth Stevens Children's Books edition

Edited, designed, and produced by
Gareth Stevens Children's Books 31 Newington Green, London N16 9PU

First published in the United States and Canada in 1988 by Gareth Stevens, Inc.
First published in the United Kingdom in 1989 by Gareth Stevens Children's Books

Cover photography courtesy of NASA

Designer: Laurie Shock
Picture research: Kathy Keller
Artwork commissioning: Kathy Keller and Laurie Shock
Project editors: Mark Sachner and Rhoda Sherwood
Editor (UK): Dee Turner

Technical advisers and consulting editors: Greg Walz-Chojnacki and Julian Baum

1 2 3 4 5 6 7 8 9 93 92 91 90 89

CONTENTS

Introduction

The Universe we live in is an enormously large place. Only in the last 50 years or so have we learned how large it really is.

It's only natural that we would want to understand the place we live in, so in the last 50 years we have developed new instruments that help us understand it. We have probes, satellites, radio telescopes, and many other things that tell us far more about the Universe than could possibly be imagined when I was young.

Nowadays, we have seen close-up pictures of the planets. We have learned about quasars and pulsars, about black holes and supernovas. We have come up with fascinating ideas about how the Universe may have come into being and how it may end. Nothing can be more astonishing and more interesting.

But of all the portions of the Universe we see in the sky, surely the most spectacular is the Sun. When it is in the sky, it drowns out everything else. It is so bright, we cannot look at it directly. In fact, we had better not try, because it can quickly damage our eyes.

When it shines, all is bright and we can see. When clouds cover it, the day turns gloomy. At night, when it is not overhead, the sky is dark. Then, unless we have artificial light, the world seems strange and dangerous. So let's learn more about our star, the Sun.

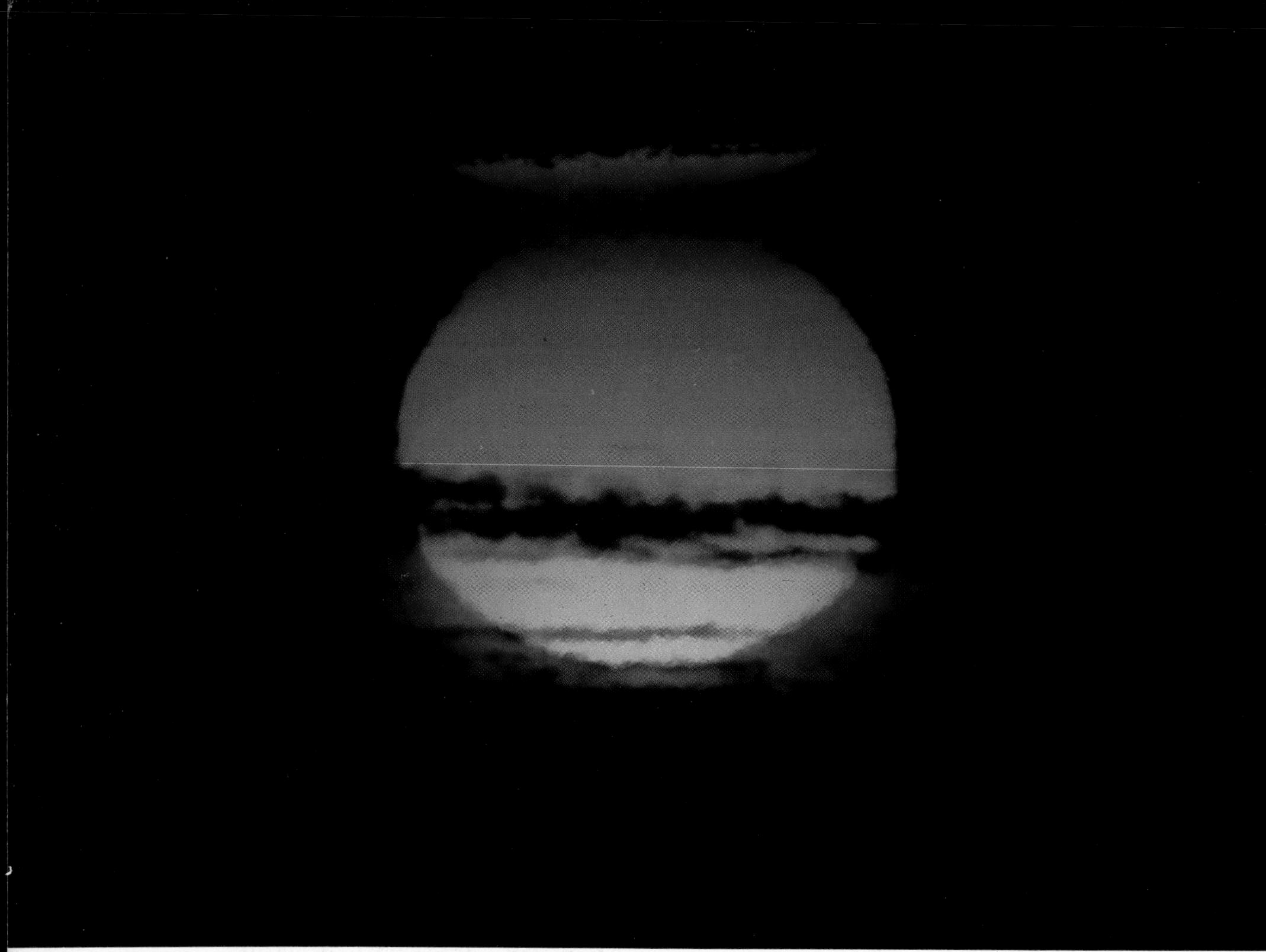

Heat! Light! Energy! The Sun supplies many of life's basic needs. The beauty of the sunrise each morning is an extra gift.

The Birth of the Sun

How did our Sun come to be? According to scientists, about five billion years ago a huge cloud of dust and gas swirled in the Universe. Perhaps a star nearby exploded, and the gases driving out of the star pushed this cloud together. The cloud started to contract. Then its own gravity made it continue to contract. As it contracted, it grew hotter and hotter. Finally, the centre of the cloud became so hot that the material in it began to change. These changes produced still more heat. The centre of the cloud 'caught fire' and became the Sun. Groups of material on the outer rim of the cloud contracted on their own and became the different planets in our Solar system.

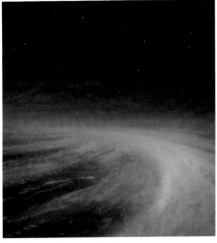

1. A great cloud of gas and dust in a sunless sky.

2. A nearby star explodes in a stupendous supernova.

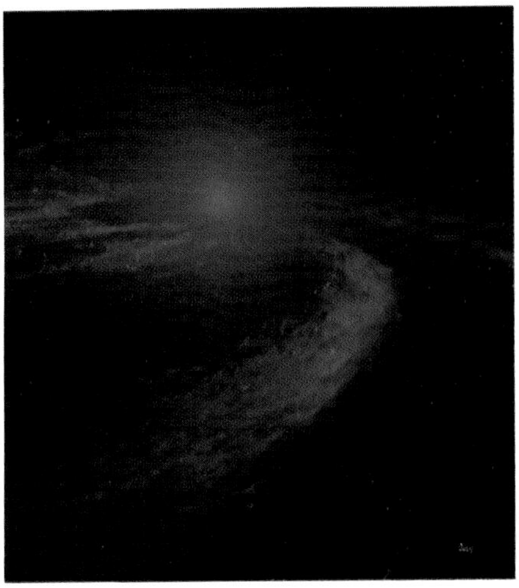

3. The cloud begins to contract. Its centre glows.

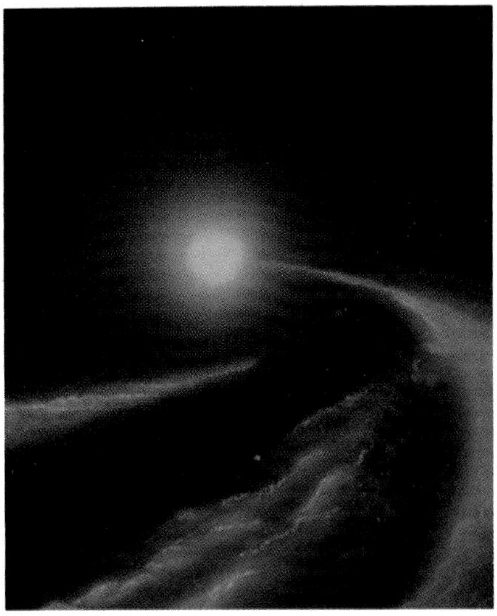

4. The centre heats up and the cloud flattens out.

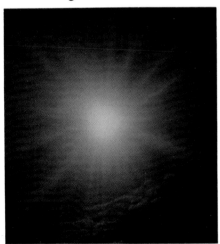

5. The centre erupts, and the Sun is born!

6. The planets calmly orbit the Sun as we know it today.

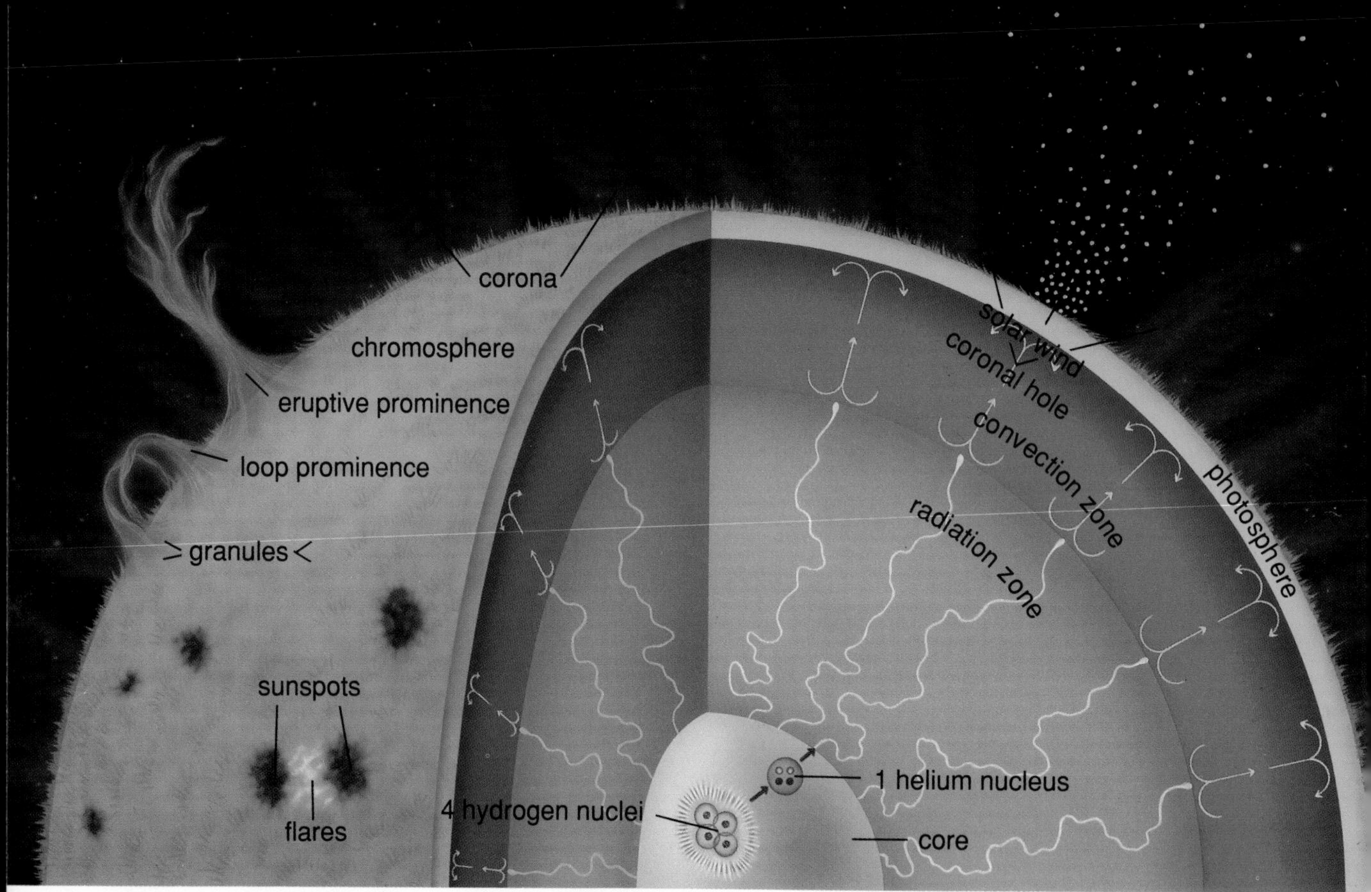

The structure of the Sun. Though gravity holds it together, the Sun has actually been exploding for billions of years. Hydrogen atoms fuse into helium, releasing energy that makes its way out of the centre as light and heat.

From H-Bombs to Sunlight

What might have happened at the centre of the cloud to make the Sun catch fire? To understand, let's compare the Sun to a hydrogen bomb. In a hydrogen bomb, heat develops. This forces atoms of hydrogen to smash into each other and cling together, or fuse, forming helium. This fusion produces enormous energies. Well, the Sun is about three-quarters hydrogen. The Sun's centre is so hot that the hydrogen fuses into helium. This creates the energy that leaks out of the Sun's surface as light and heat. We might say the Sun is a huge hydrogen bomb that has been exploding for billions of years. Fortunately, the Sun's gravity holds it together and keeps the explosion from going out of control.

We could call the Sun a naturally occurring hydrogen bomb. Here is an unnaturally occurring hydrogen bomb — one made by humans as a weapon.

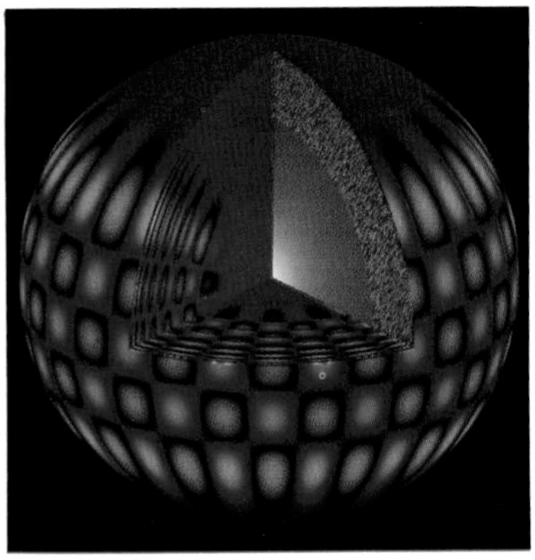

A computer made this picture to show how the Sun oscillates, or wavers. The reds show regions moving back. The blues show regions moving forward. Pictures like this help scientists learn about the structure and inside activity of the Sun.

The case of the missing neutrinos

When hydrogen fuses to make helium deep in the Sun's centre it produces some very tiny particles called neutrinos. These are hard to detect. But in the 1970s an American scientist, Raymond Davis, worked out a way. He tried to trap at least a few neutrinos that came from the Sun. He didn't expect many, but the number he got was only one-third the number he had expected to get!
The experiment has been repeated over and over, and each time there is a neutrino shortage. Why? Do scientists have the wrong idea about what goes on inside the Sun? It's just not clear.

A neutrino detector. This instrument allows scientists to trap and count neutrinos.

Ruler of the Solar System

Our brilliant star, the Sun, is huge. It is about 150 million km away from us. So it must be huge to be seen, at that distance in the sky, as such a large ball. It is about 1,390,000 km across, 108 times as wide as Earth. It has 333,400 times the mass of Earth. In fact, it has almost 1,000 times the combined mass of all the planets, satellites, asteroids, and comets circling it! The Sun's gravitational pull is so strong that it holds all those objects and forces them to move around it. Our Earth is one of those planets revolving around the Sun, making one complete circle in a year.

The Sun erupting. The size of the Earth as shown in this picture gives you an idea of how huge Solar eruptions can be. If we could harness the energy from an eruption like this, we would have enough power for all human needs for the next 2,000 years. This eruption occurred on June 10, 1973, and was recorded by Skylab 2.

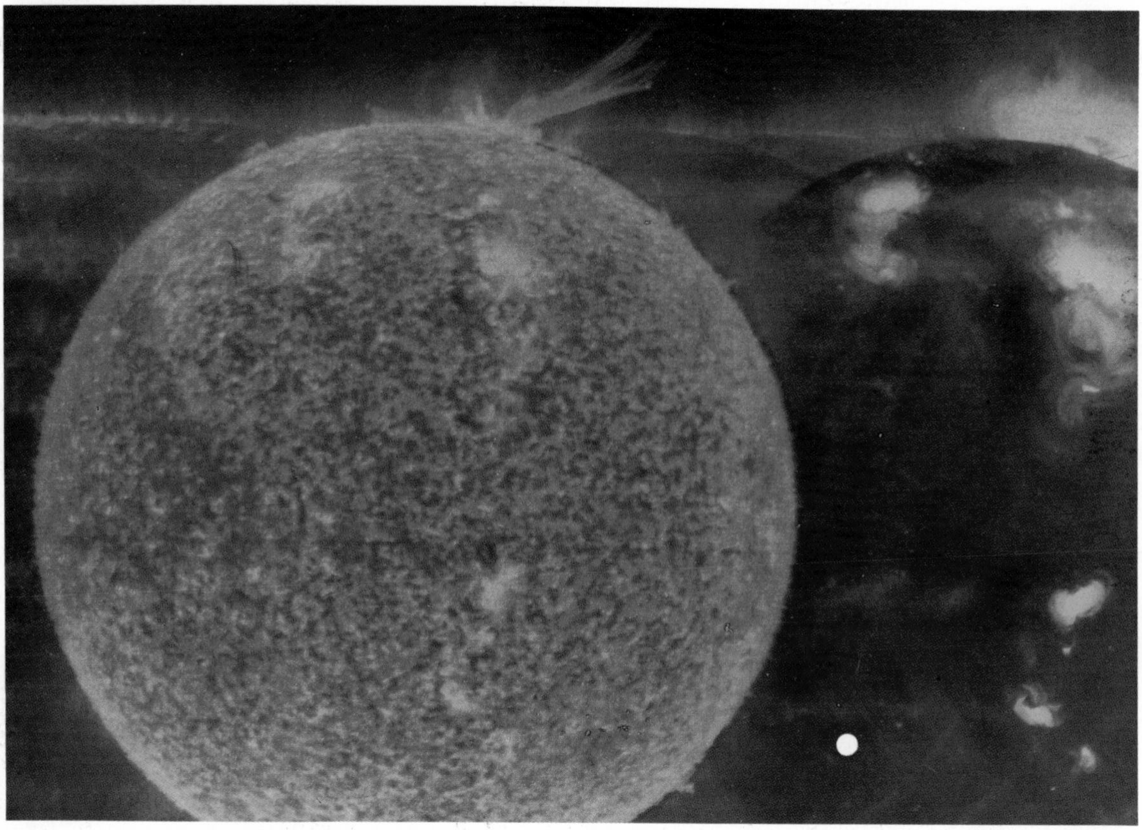

Our Earth-Moon system — tiny beside the Sun!

Here's one way to think about the Sun's size. Imagine that Earth is placed in the centre of the Sun. Also imagine that the Moon is circling the Earth at its usual distance of 384,321 km. The Moon, as it circled, would still be inside the Sun. In fact, it would be only a little over halfway to the Sun's surface. In other words, the Sun alone is bigger than the entire Earth-Moon system! Astronauts have travelled from Earth to the Moon, but they have not yet gone far enough to match the distance from the Sun's centre to the Sun's surface.

As Earth revolves, or orbits, around the Sun, the northern and southern ends of Earth's axis take turns tilting toward the Sun. Summer comes to the hemisphere that tilts toward the Sun; winter comes to the hemisphere that tilts away from the Sun. The amount of time it takes Earth to complete its orbit is of special importance to us. We call it a year.

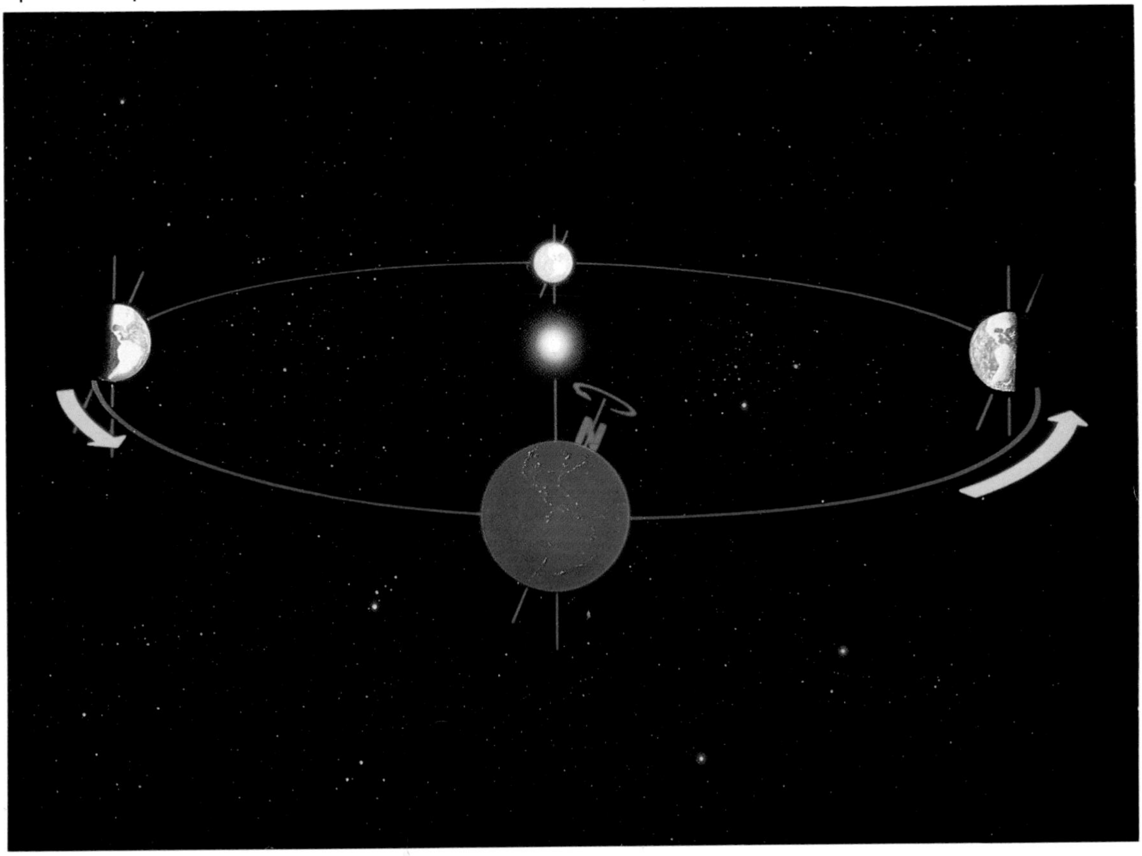

Our Star, the Sun

Why do we need this powerful star? In ancient times, at night when the Sun was not in the sky, our world was dark except for the dim light of a campfire or the Moon. It was also cold, especially in the winter and especially when the campfire burned low. How relieved people were when the Sun finally rose! Then the light came, and the Earth grew warm again.

Ra, the Sun god of ancient Egyptian mythology, was usually shown with a hawk's head on a human body. He controlled the Universe by rowing the Sun across the sky in his boat, taking the world from day to night and back to day again. Many ancient religions felt that the creation of the world was made possible by the power of the Sun and its gods.

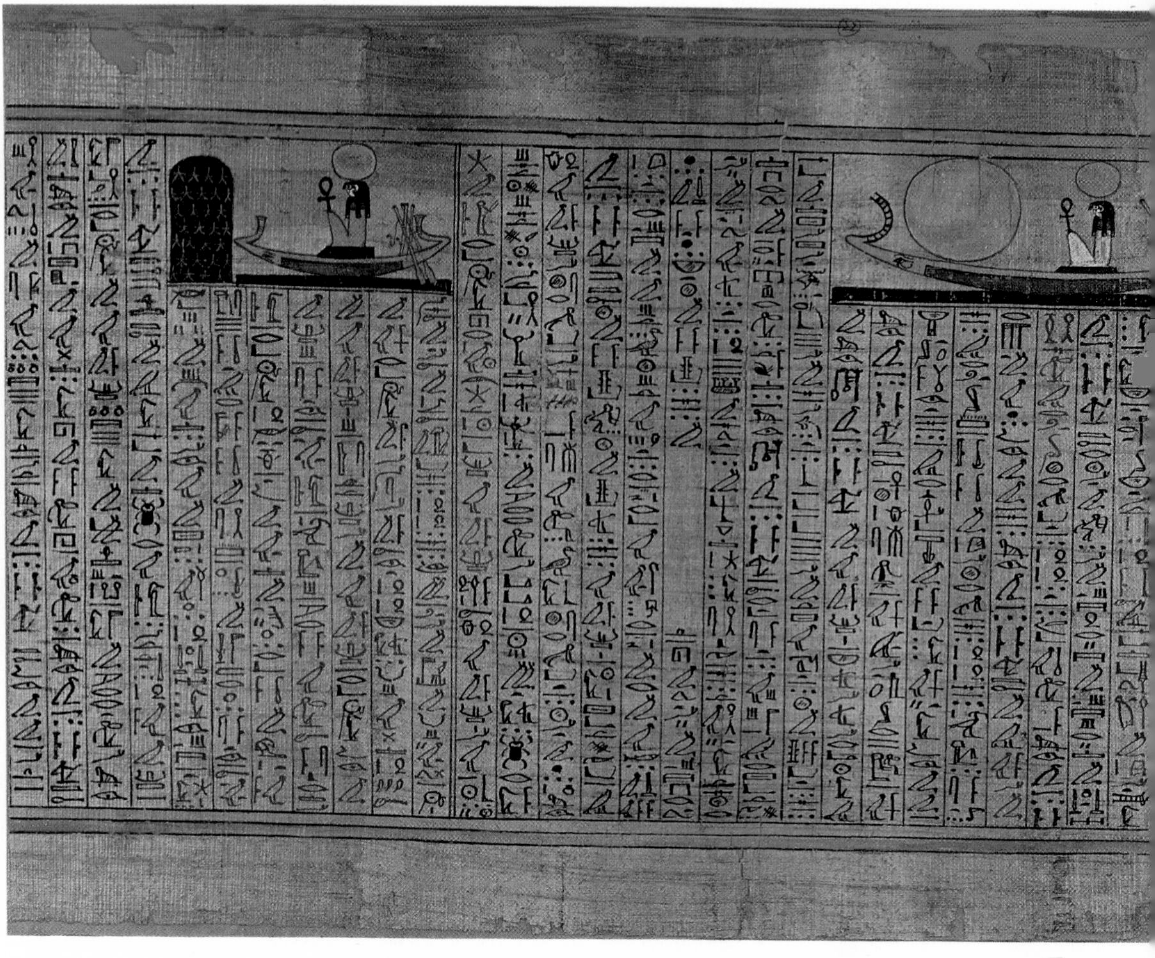

When you think about the Sun's light and warmth, it's no wonder many primitive people worshipped it as a god. They had good reason to. Without the Sun, everything would freeze, plants would not grow, animals would not have food. Without the Sun, in fact, there would be no life on Earth.

Our Sun: not too big, not too small — just right!

The more massive a star, the shorter its lifetime. A massive star has more hydrogen to undergo fusion and produce energy. But the hydrogen in a massive star must fuse very rapidly to produce the energy to keep the star from collapsing under its own gravitational pull. An extremely massive star might survive only 100 million years. Then it would explode and collapse. That's not enough time for life to develop. A very small star, on the other hand, might last 200 billion years. But a small star wouldn't produce enough energy for life to develop. Our middle-sized star, the Sun, is just right. It not only produces enough energy for life but also will survive for a total of 10 billion years. This gives the time needed for life to form.

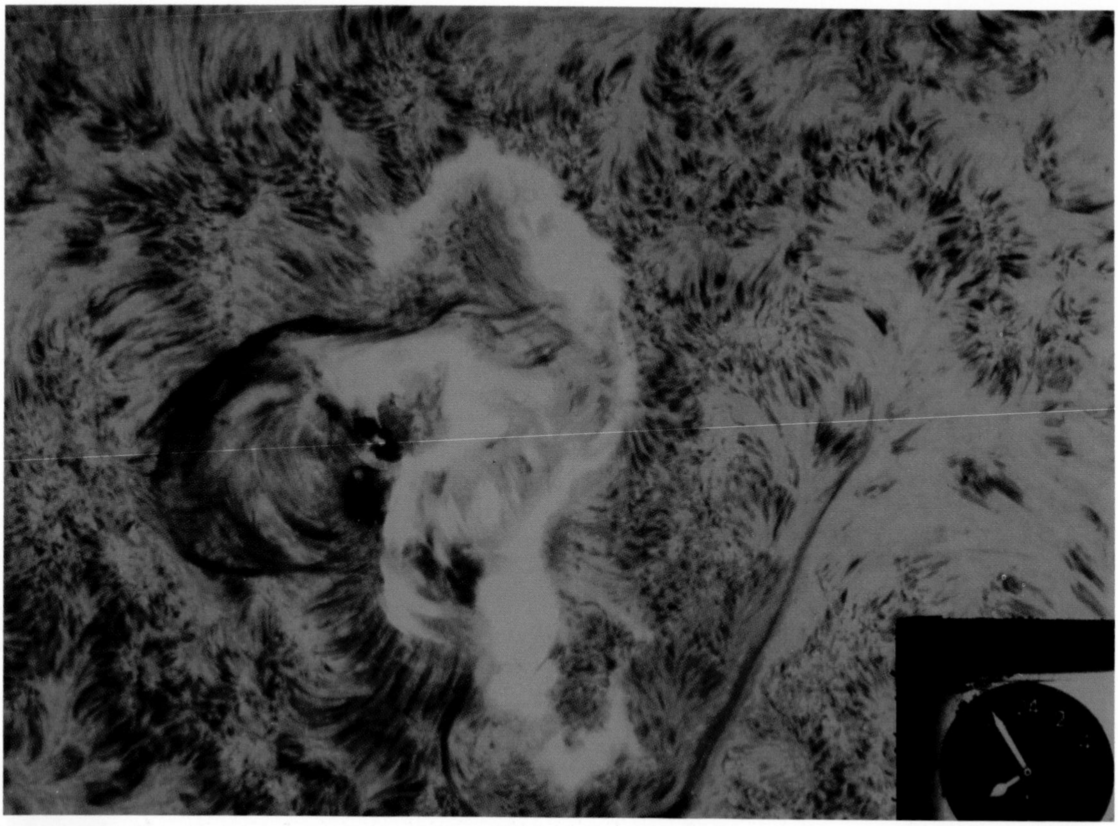

The swirling waves on the Sun mean that the Sun's surface rises and sinks. The wavy surface of the Sun is made up of granules that come and go like bubbles in boiling water. Each granule has about an eight-minute existence.

The Sun's Surface: Waves of Grain

The Sun's surface is not even. Parts of it are always rising, and other parts are sinking. It's a little bit like the water of Earth's oceans that rises and falls in waves. As a result of this rising and sinking, the surface of the Sun seems to consist of grains or granules made of cells of matter packed closely together. Each grain looks small to us on Earth, but on the average it is about 1,000 km across! Although large, a granule does not live long. Each lasts about eight minutes. Then a new one forms, just as bubbles keep on replacing one another in a pan of boiling water. Scientists think that there are about four million granules on the Sun's surface at any one time!

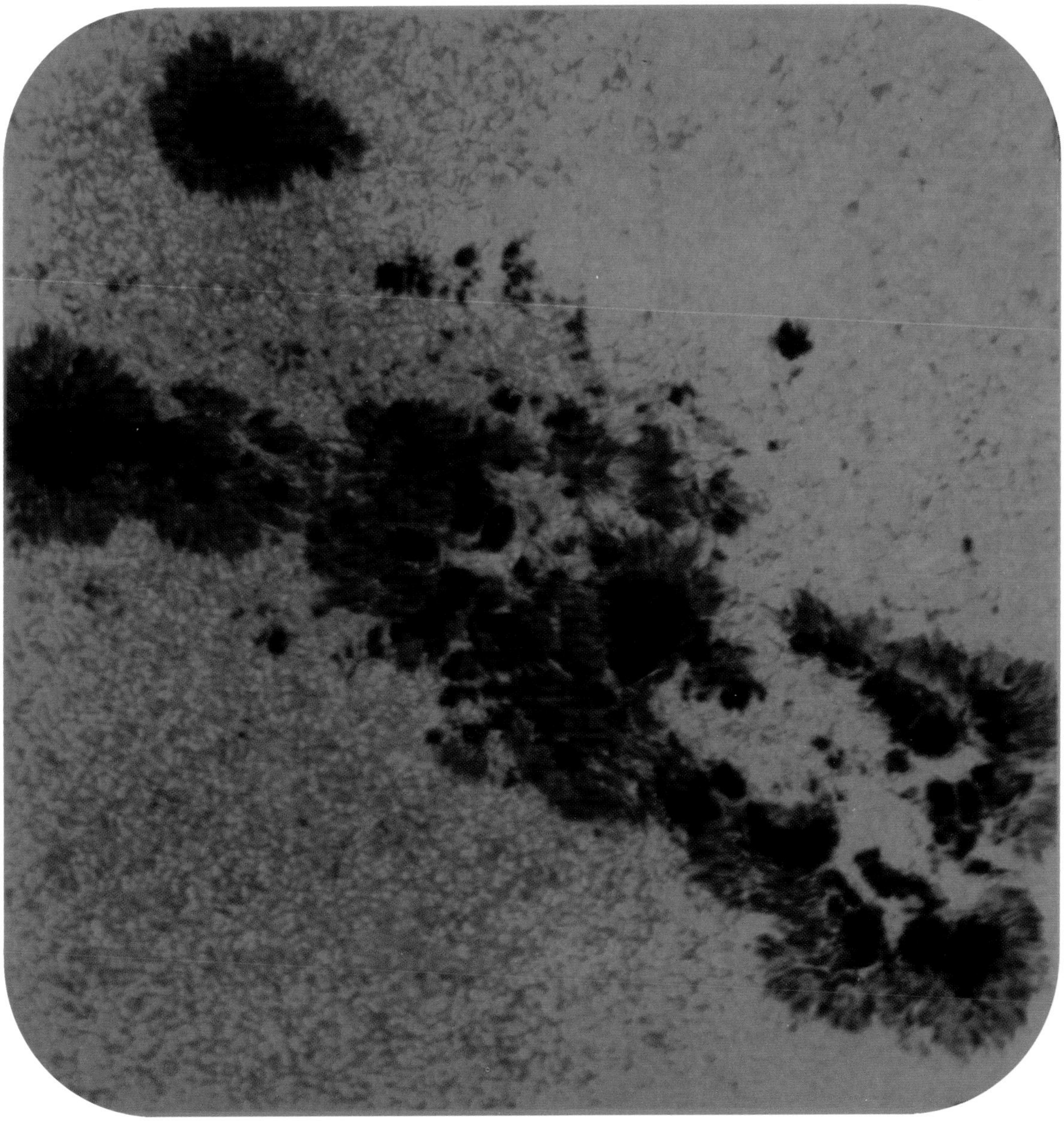

In this picture, small granules surround the large dark sunspots. The Sun's granules may look small, but each of those 'tiny' grains averages about 1,000 km in diameter.

Spots and Flares

The temperature at the Sun's surface is 5,500° C. At the centre, the temperature is about 14,000,000° C. But this central heat leaks outward only very slowly. On the Sun's surface this heat energy is very active. Here and there, the hot gases expand and become cooler. The cooler gases shine less brightly than the hot gases do, so some areas are dark. A dark region is a sunspot. The number of sunspots on the Sun varies. Some years there are over 100 sunspots, and in some years there are fewer than 10.

In areas around sunspots, the gases are more active. Explosions near these spots give off a lot of energy. When waves from the explosions hit Earth, they even affect compasses on planes and ships! These explosions, called flares, also shine brightly. So while the sunspots are somewhat cooler — around 4,500° C — the flares are hot and more than make up for sunspots. When the Sun is particularly spotty, Earth is also a bit warmer than at other times.

Images of a bipolar sunspot, recorded on February 13, 1978. A bipolar sunspot has north and south magnetic poles. Left: a magnetogram, showing the magnetic fields. Yellow indicates north; purple, south. Centre: a white light photograph. Right: The yellow in this picture shows material flowing away from Earth out of the sunspot. Blue indicates material flowing toward Earth.

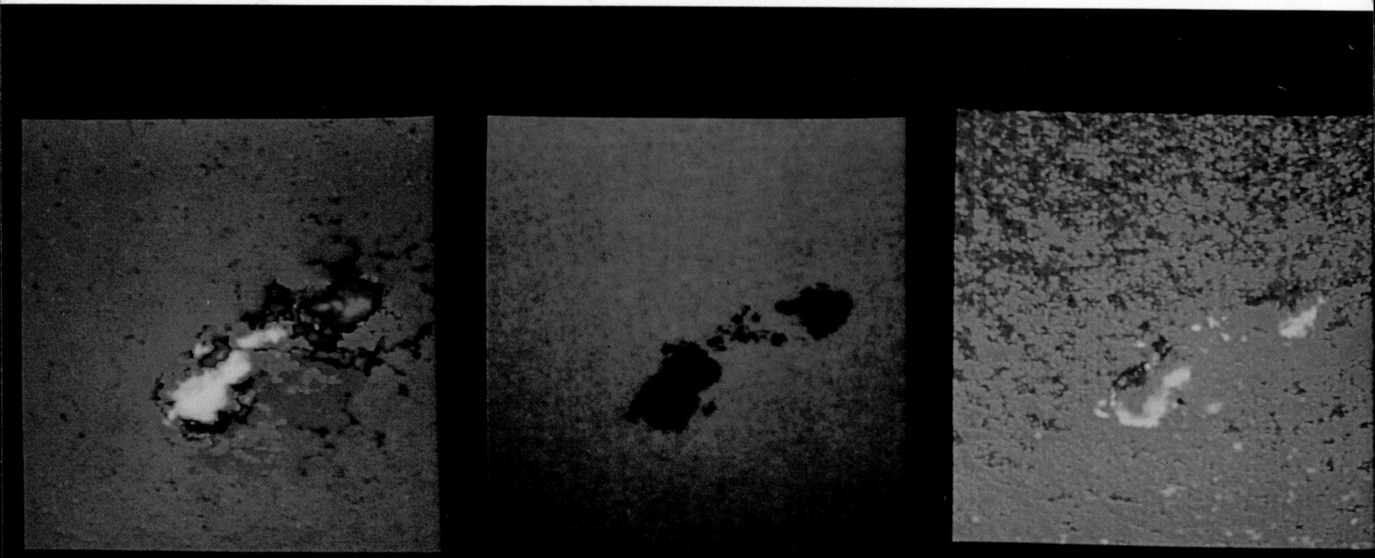

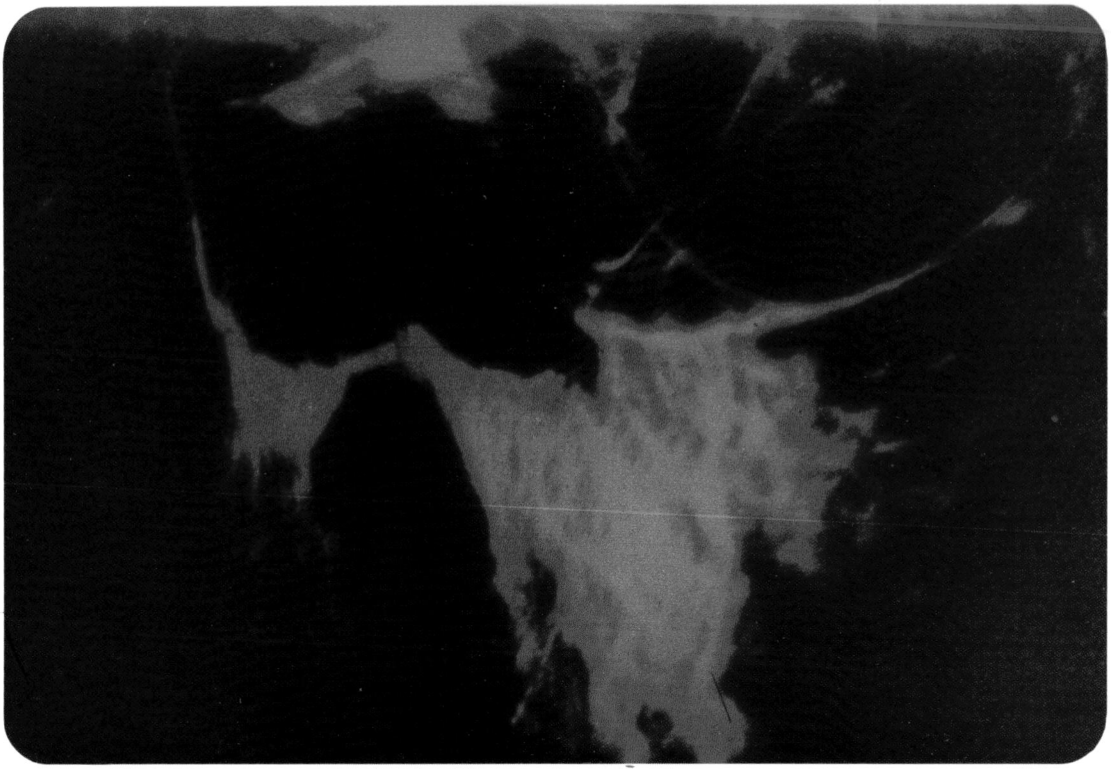

The enormous power of Solar flares can even reach to Earth, distorting compass readings on planes and ships.

The hotter gases on the Sun's surface shine more brightly than the cooler gases. The cooler gases form dark areas — sunspots. In this picture, the bright flashes are flares.

A rare spiral-shaped sunspot, February 19, 1982. Normally, sunspots are seen as irregularly shaped dark holes. This unusual sunspot had a diameter six times that of Earth!

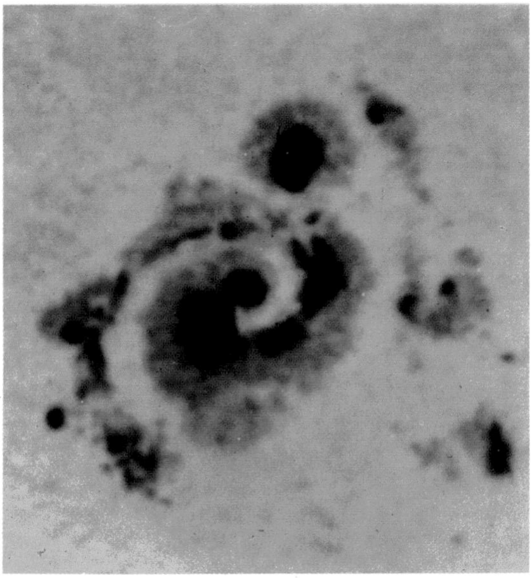

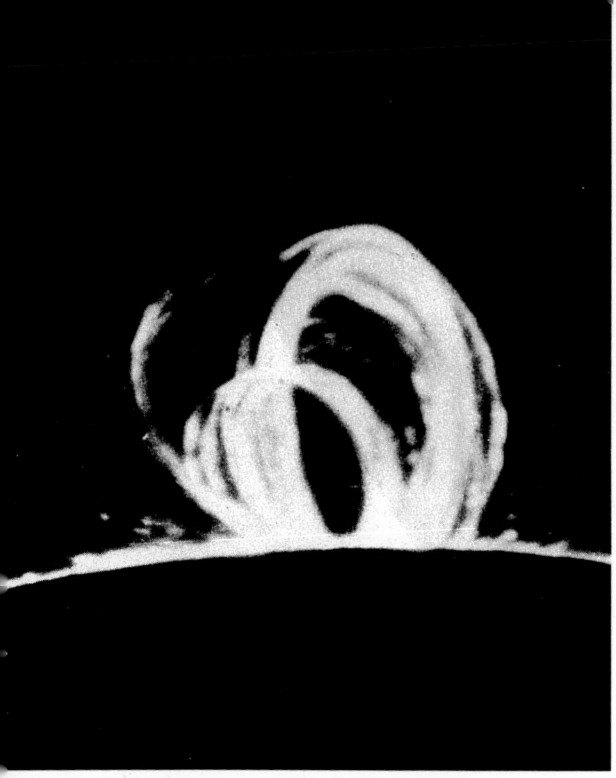

The face, or photosphere, of the Sun with prominences.

Photographing prominences requires a longer exposure than photographing the Sun itself. That is why photographers often mask out the Sun so they can record the prominence without overexposing the whole whole picture.

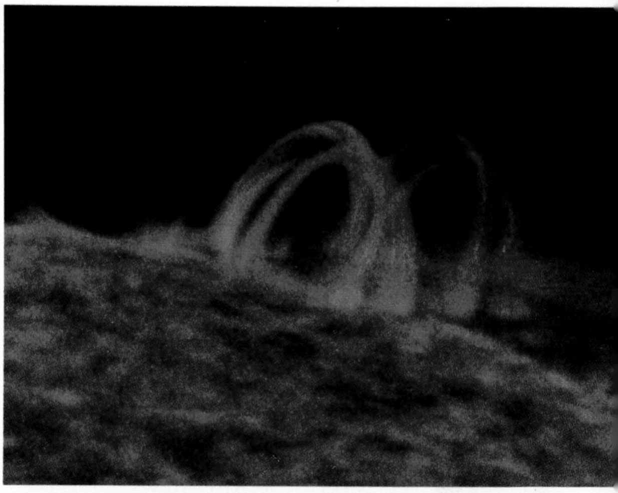

The Sun's photosphere with loop prominences. The shape of loop prominences is caused by strong magnetic fields that bend the hot gases into a loop. The prominences hold hot, electrically charged gases above the Sun's active regions.

Ribbons of Gas

Between sunspots are dark ribbons, or filaments, which are called prominences. Like sunspots, prominences are made of cooler gases. Scientists think these prominences occur just before flares become active. The prominences lift off the Sun's surface and erupt through its thin outer atmosphere, called the corona. The gases of the corona glow with red light and then sink down to the surface of the Sun. We can see these ribbons of gas with special instruments. When looked at straight on, these ribbons look like dark filaments. But coming off the edge of the Sun, they form graceful arches, tens of thousands of kilometres high.

The longest spike, or streamer, in this picture projects more than 1.61 million km beyond the Sun's surface. Just after this coronagraph was taken, a Solar flare erupted on the right edge of the Sun. Within minutes the corona changed its shape.

Does the Sun influence the Earth?

Does the Sun influence the Earth? Of course it does. It gives us light and warmth. But what about the sunspot cycle? Every 11 years, the Sun gets very spotty at sunspot maximum and almost clear at sunspot minimum. That means the Sun gets a trifle warmer and then a trifle cooler. Does this affect Earth's temperature, its harvests, its rainfall? Possibly. Some people even think that the sunspot cycle might affect stock market prices, the ups and downs of the economy, and so on. It seems hard to believe — but is it possible?

Skylab took this coronagraph of the Sun in 1974. That day the emissions beyond the Sun's corona extended for millions of kilometres.

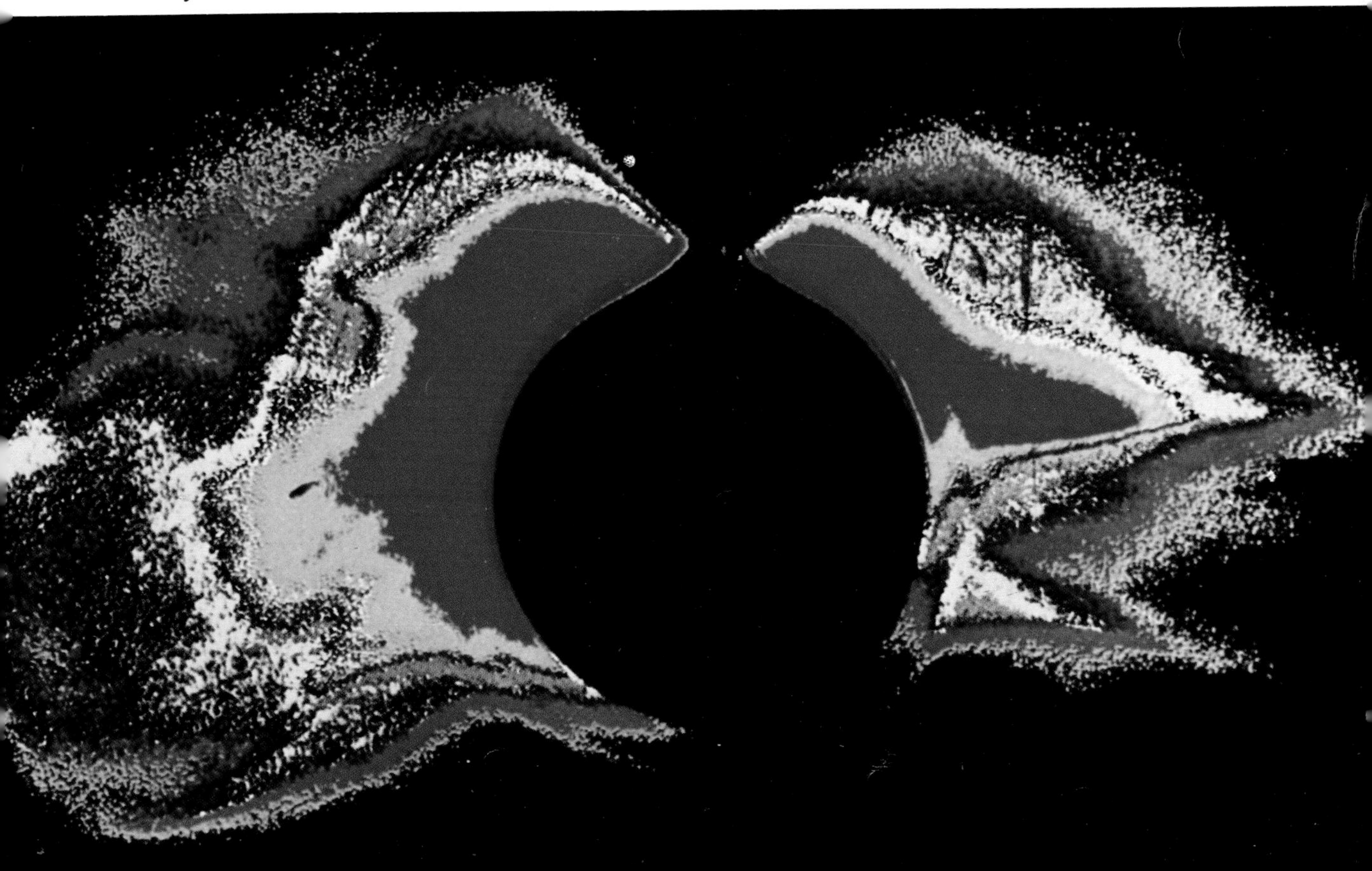

The aurora is a common sight over Canada or Alaska, USA. But this picture is unusual because it was taken in Arizona, where the sight of the aurora is quite rare. Shown here beneath the aurora is the Kitt Peak National Observatory.

The Sunlight of Night

All this activity on the Sun's surface sends tiny particles outward in all directions. These particles carry electric charges and travel at a speed of about 500 km a second. This stream of particles is called the solar wind.

This wind reaches far out in space, passing by the various planets. When it reaches Earth, it strikes the upper atmosphere, particularly near the North and South Poles. The energy from this collision then releases energy in the form of light. As a result, the polar nights are lit by faint-coloured light in streamers and curves. This light is called the aurora. Sometimes, when the Sun is very active, the aurora can be seen beyond the polar regions.

Two photos of the Aurora Borealis, or Northern Lights, over Alaska. The aurora that is visible in the southern hemisphere is called Aurora Australis.

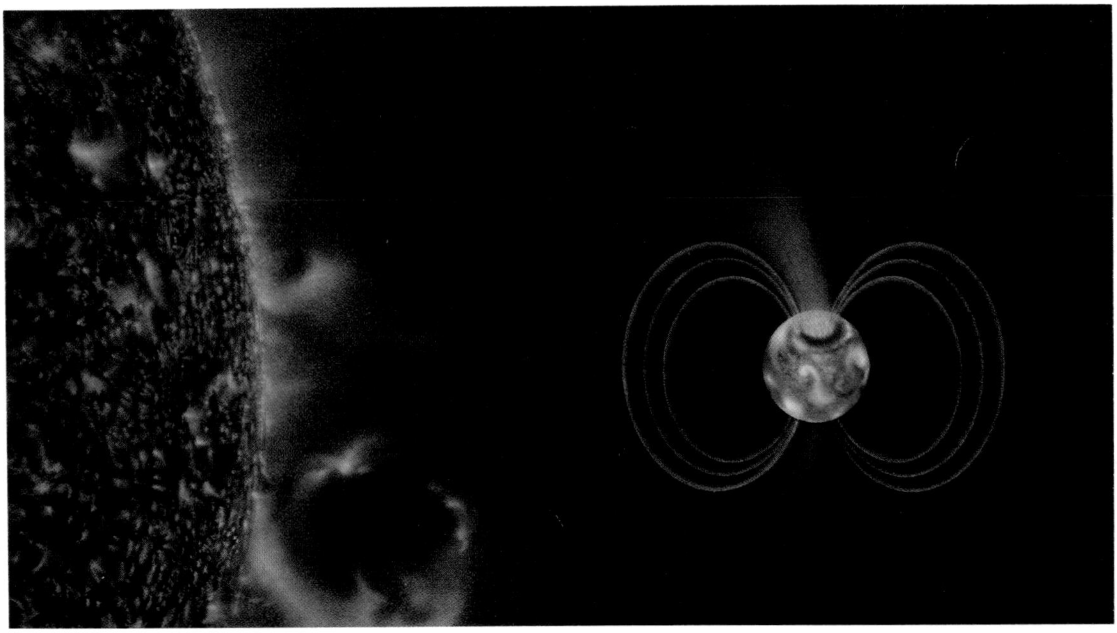

An illustration showing the Sun and Earth's magnetosphere. The magnetosphere shields Earth from the solar wind. But, as the picture shows, it also allows the solar wind into the upper atmosphere over the North and South Poles.

Daytime Night

Our Moon has helped us learn about the Sun — without our even leaving Earth. Sometimes the Sun seems to grow dark in the middle of a cloudless sky. This is because the Moon occasionally moves directly between us and the Sun. The Moon can block the entire body of the Sun. But the Sun's corona shines softly as a kind of halo around the Moon. This blocking is a total solar eclipse. It can last up to seven and a half minutes, at the most, before part of the Sun shows again. Each year there are from two to five partial eclipses. Since the Moon's shadow falls over only a small part of Earth in one eclipse, people in any one area on Earth see a total solar eclipse only about once every 300 years.

A 1970 solar eclipse passes by a tracking station at Wallops Island, Virginia, USA.

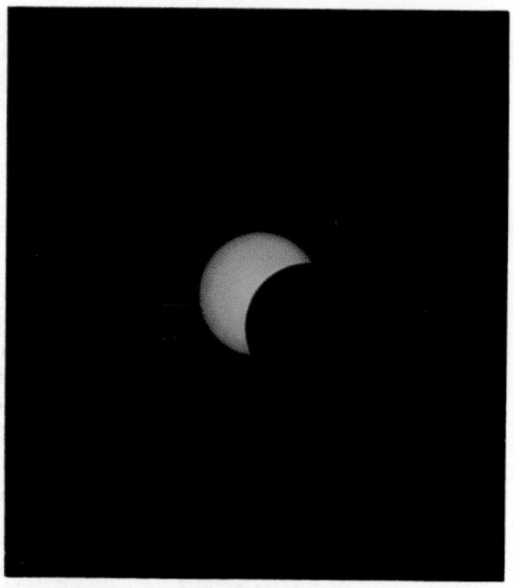

A partial eclipse of the Sun: The Moon is moving across the Sun's face.

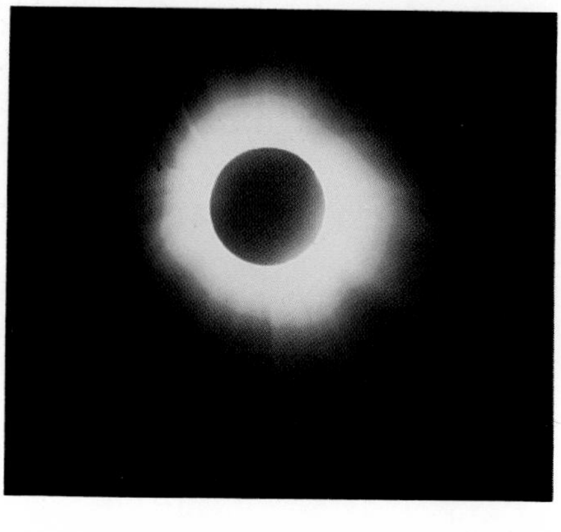

A total eclipse of the Sun: Only the Sun's corona is visible.

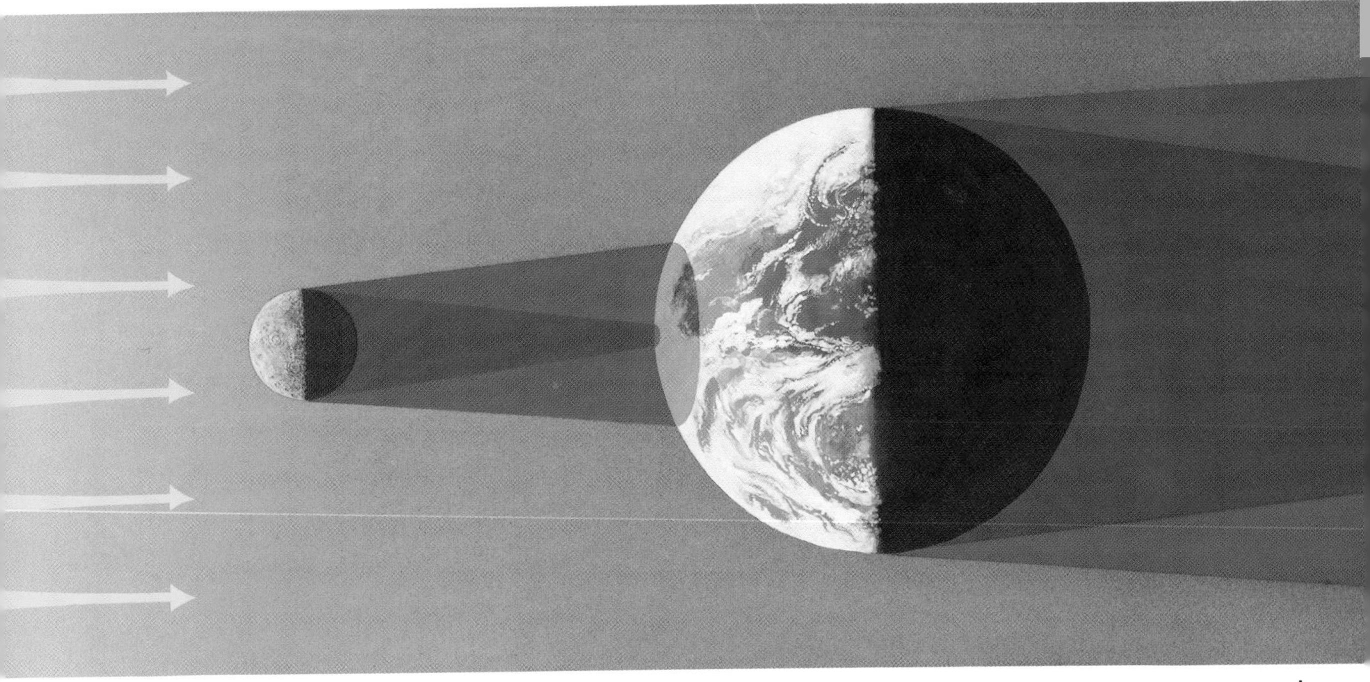

During a total eclipse of the Sun, the Moon blocks out the Sun's light from part of Earth. Within the smallest circle in this picture, the sky would be quite dark and a person's view of the Sun would be that of the total eclipse. People within the outer circle would find daylight to be a strange kind of shadow and the Sun only partially eclipsed by the Moon.

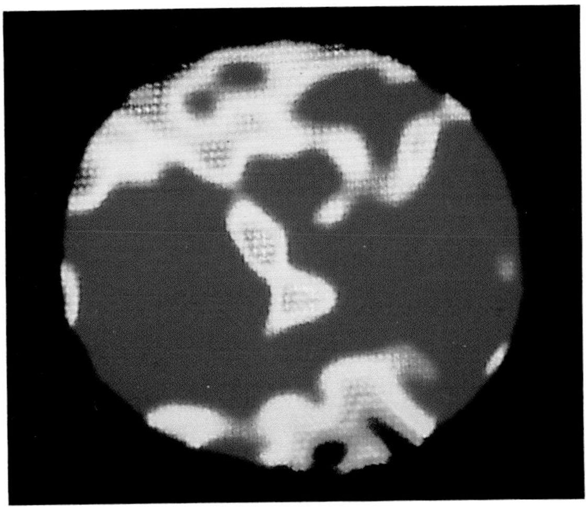

Many photographic images were taken and combined to produce this single computer-generated image of the giant Betelgeuse.

The red giants — big, bigger, biggest

As large as the Sun is, it is not the largest star. There are stars called red giants that are so huge they stretch across six to eight hundred million km. Imagine that the Sun was in the centre of a red giant — such as the one named Betelgeuse. That red giant would stretch out past the Earth and maybe even past Mars! Of course, red giant stars have their material spread out very thinly. But even so, Betelgeuse is 18 times as massive as the Sun. There are other stars that are 90 to 100 times as massive as the Sun.

New Ways to View the Sun

Most of the time, we use instruments to study the Sun. Since 1814, an instrument called the spectroscope has been used to watch sunlight. It spreads out, in order of length, the tiny waves that make up light. Different wavelengths have different colours. Beginning in 1891, scientists used an instrument called a spectroheliograph to study the Sun by examining a particular wavelength. This helped tell them what elements made up the Sun. And since 1931, we haven't had to wait for an eclipse to look directly at the Sun. Since then, even when there is no eclipse, scientists have used the coronagraph to cover the Sun and study the corona.

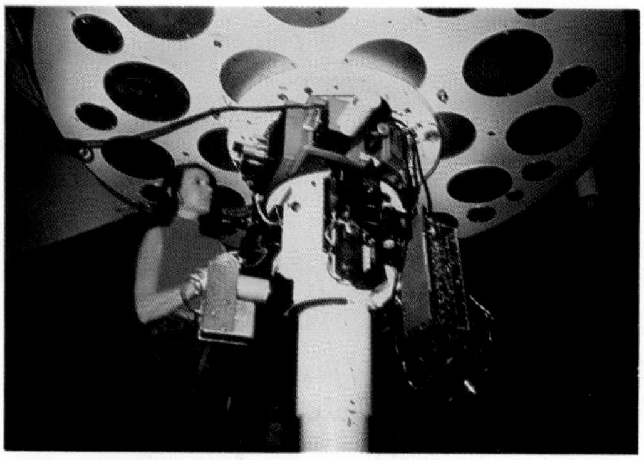

An astronomer at Kitt Peak examines a spectroheliograph attached to a telescope.

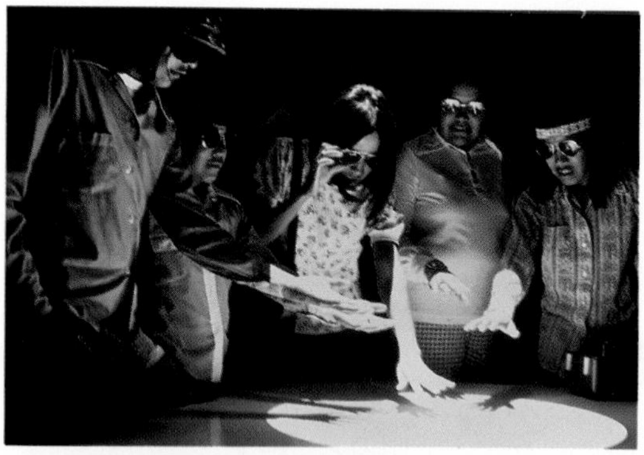

Navajo students examine a Solar image in the McMath Solar Telescope at Kitt Peak. The McMath gives the largest, clearest image of our Sun.

A sunspot shot taken at Kitt Peak in the USA. On the right, a white, or natural, light shot of the sunspot. On the left, a spectrum shot of the same area.

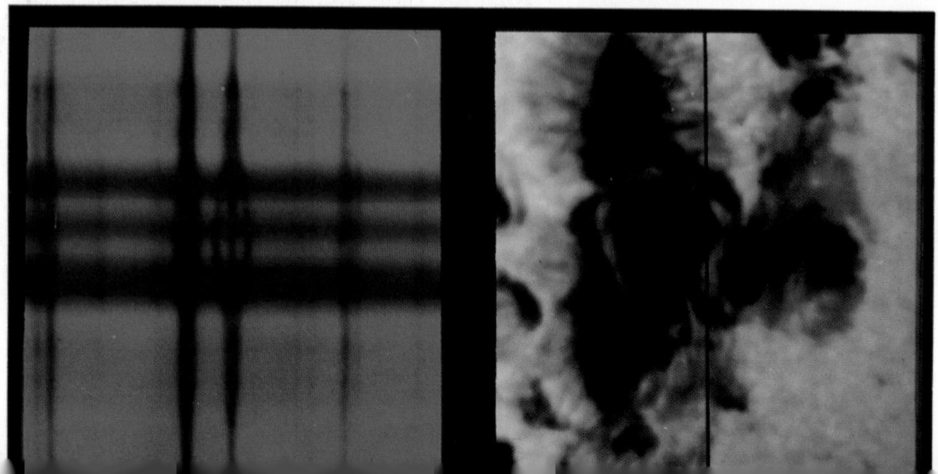

Solar spectrum: The visible or white light portion of the spectrum of the Sun has been split into all its colours in this spectrogram.

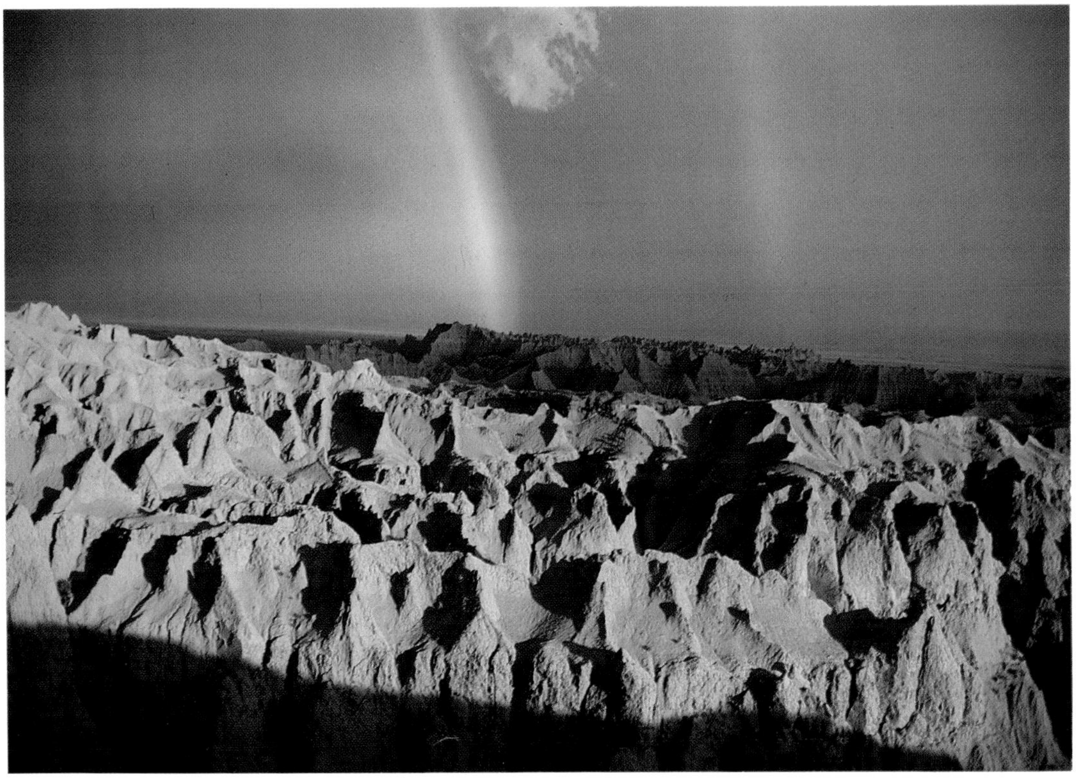

A rainbow — a naturally occurring spectrogram!

Skylab 3: This view of Skylab in Earth orbit was taken from the Command/Service Module during a 'fly around' inspection of the orbiting satellite. Earth's clouds and water are visible far below.

The Sun from Space

Other tools help us see the Sun from outside our atmosphere. Not all the radiation from the Sun reaches the Earth. The atmosphere absorbs much of the radiation before it can reach us. So there is a lot about the Sun that we cannot know from Earth.

In order to study all the radiation from the Sun, we must observe it from space, from outside the atmosphere. Special satellites have been used for such studies since 1957. Many nations have built and launched these satellites, including the US, the Soviet Union, Japan, West Germany, and India. In 1973, a satellite named Skylab carried human beings into space, where they could study the Sun's radiation. They also discovered some regions in the corona that were cool and had little gas in them. These regions are called coronal holes.

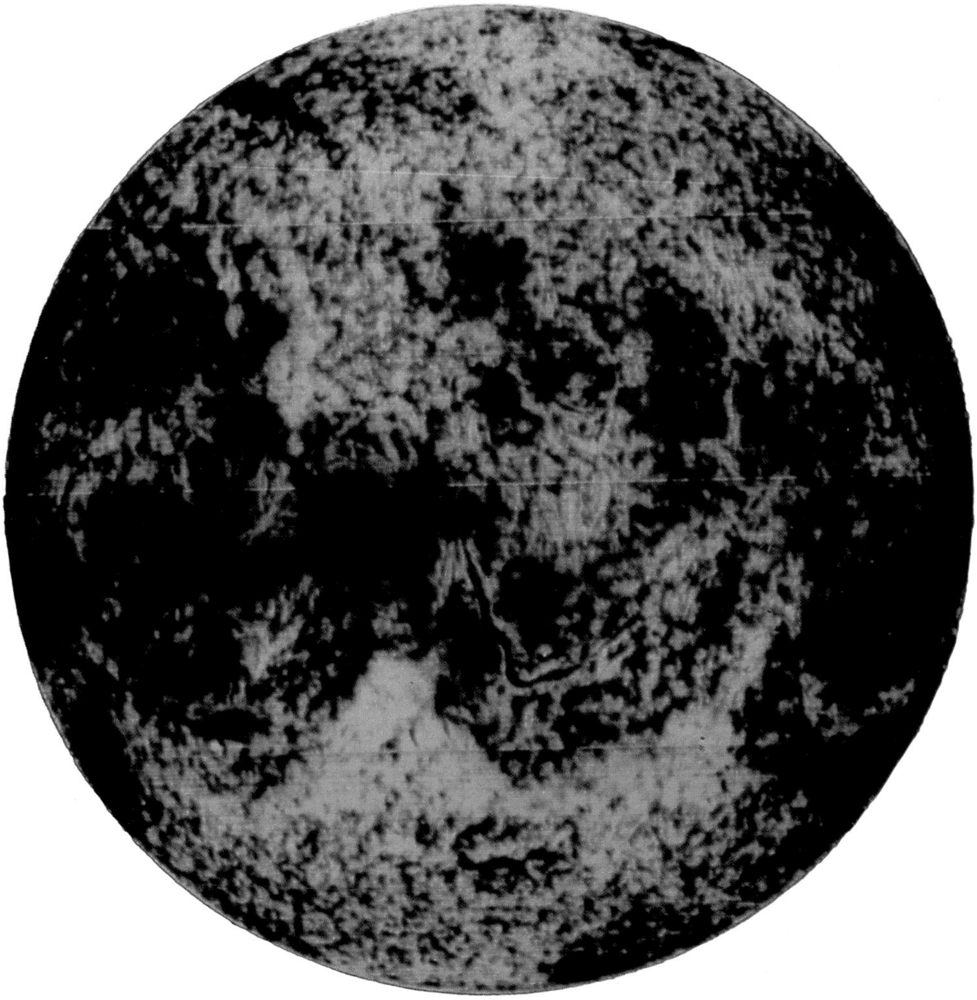

This ultraviolet picture of the Sun shows a coronal hole in the Sun's outer atmosphere. Coronal holes are believed to be the main outlet for the solar wind.

Probing the Sun's Secrets

There is still a great deal to find out about the Sun and how we can use it creatively on Earth. Scientists, for instance, continue to study the sunspot cycle — the rise and fall in the number of sunspots from year to year. If they learn why it takes place, they may learn more about what goes on deep inside the Sun.

We have learned how to harness some of the Sun's energy for heating. Many buildings have special devices that capture the Sun's rays and store their heat for later use. These devices help us conserve resources like coal and oil that are running out. Who knows what we might be able to do someday as we continue to unravel the mysteries of our star, the Sun?

Star Probe — a possible addition to Earth's fleet of space probes. It would send back new pictures and information about our star.

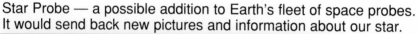

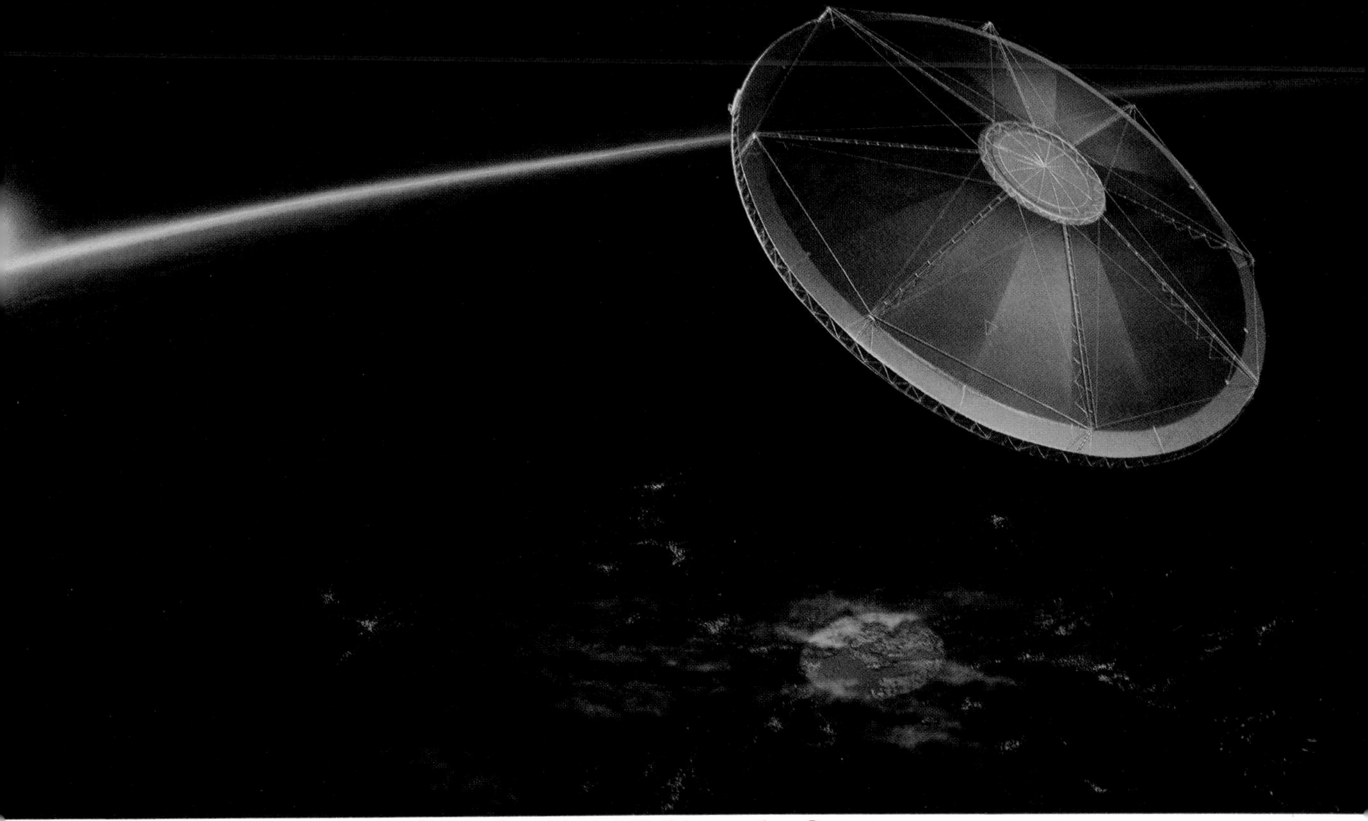

Light in an emergency: Why should nightfall keep the Sun from lighting up our lives? A huge Space Mirror satellite could reflect the Sun's light at night, providing light during a blackout. In this illustration, blacked-out New York City is the lucky recipient of emergency sunlight.

The case of the missing sunspots

It seems the sunspot cycle isn't always with us. The Italian scientist Galileo discovered sunspots in 1610. Others observed them, too. But then, between 1645 and 1715, hardly a sunspot was to be seen on the Sun. After that, the familiar sunspot cycle began. We call the spotless period between 1645 and 1715 a Maunder minimum, because an astronomer named Maunder discussed it in 1890. Apparently, there have been similar periods throughout history when sunspots were missing. What causes the cycle to suddenly stop and then restart? At the moment, astronomers aren't sure.

Fact File: The Sun

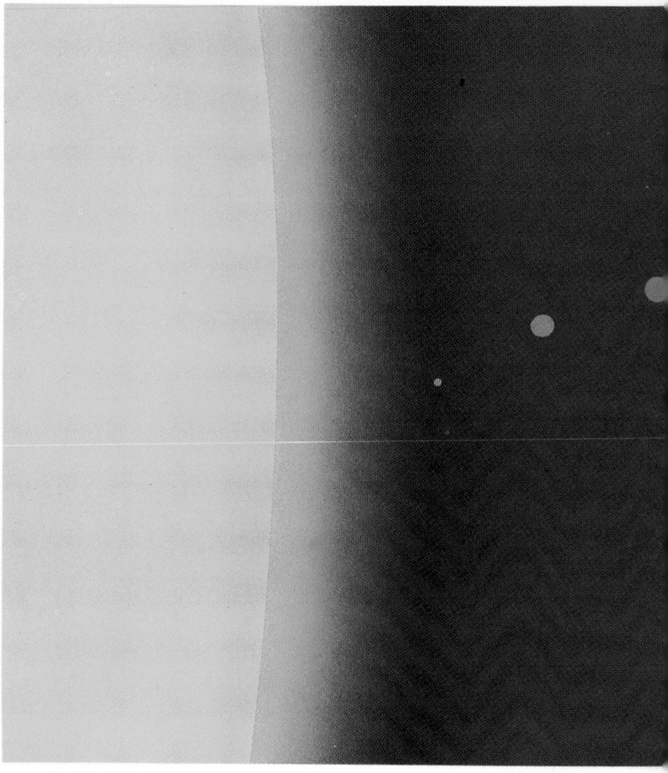

The Sun is, of course, our very own star. As far as stars go, the Sun is not all that big. But its diameter is about 108 times bigger than that of Earth. And it is about 270,000 times closer to Earth than is Alpha Centauri, the next closest star. So it looks quite big to us here on Earth. While the light from Alpha Centauri takes over four years to reach Earth, the light from the Sun takes only about eight minutes. So, though the Sun is small compared to many stars, its size and distance from Earth enabled life to develop on our planet.

Here is a close-up of the Sun and some of its special features, as well as some fascinating comparisons between our star and our planet, Earth.

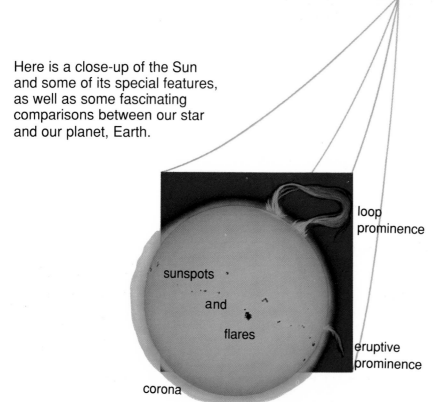

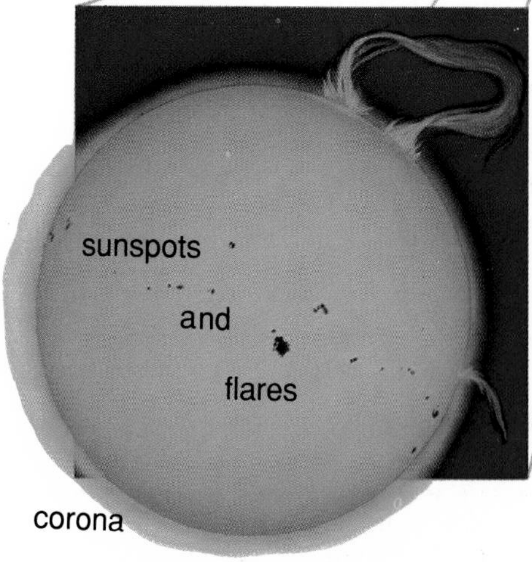

Object	Diameter
Sun	864,988 miles (1,392,000 km
Earth	7,927 miles (12,756 km)

The Sun and Its Family of Planets

The Sun and its Solar system family, left to right: Mercury, Venus, Earth, Mars, Jupiter, Saturn, Uranus, Neptune, Pluto.

The Sun: How It Measures Up

Rotation Period (length of day)	Period of Orbit Around Sun (length of year)	Surface Gravity	Distance from Sun (nearest-farthest)	Least Time It Takes for Light to Travel to Earth
25-35 days	—	27.9*	—	8.3 minutes
23 hours, 56 minutes	365.25 days (one year)	1.00*	91-95 million miles (147-152 million km)	—

* Multiply your weight by this number to find out how much you would weigh on the Sun or Earth.

More Books About the Sun

Here are more books that contain information about the Sun and its neighbourhood, the Solar system. If you are interested in them, look for them in your library or bookshop.

Astronomy by Ed Catherall (Wayland, 1986)
Discovering Astronomy by Jacqueline and Simon Mitton (Longman, 1979)
Our Solar System by Isaac Asimov (Gareth Stevens, 1989)
The Planets by Michael Jay (Franklin Watts, 1982)
Solar System by Sue Becklake (Macmillan Children's Books, 1987)
The Sun by Heather Couper (Franklin Watts, 1985)
Sun, Moon and Planets by Lynn Myring (Usborne, 1982)
Sun and Stars by Norman Barrett (Franklin Watts, 1985)
The Young Astronomer's Handbook by Ian Ridpath (Hamlyn, 1981)

Places to Visit

You can explore the Universe — including the Sun and our Solar system — without leaving Earth. Here are some museums and centres where you can find many different kinds of space exhibits.

London Schools Planetarium
Wandsworth School,
Sutherland Grove,
London

London Planetarium
Marylebone Road,
London

Royal Greenwich Observatory
Herstmonceux Castle
Hailsham, E. Sussex

Jodrell Bank Visitors' Centre
Macclesfield, Cheshire

Science Museum
S. Kensington, London

Royal Observatory
Edinburgh, Scotland

There are also planetaria at museums in Southend, Liverpool, National Maritime Museum (Greenwich, London), Armagh Observatory (N. Ireland), and Mills Observatory, Dundee (Scotland).

For More Information About the Sun

Here are some people you can write to for more information about the Sun. Be sure to tell them exactly what you want to know about. And include your age, full name, and address so they can write back to you.

For information about the Sun:
STARDATE
MacDonald Observatory
Austin, Texas 78712, USA

For astro-photography of the Sun:
Caltech Bookstore
California Institute of Technology
Mail Code 1-51
Pasadena, California 91125, USA

Glossary

asteroids: very small planets made of rock or metal. There are thousands of them in our Solar system, and they mainly orbit the Sun between Mars and Jupiter. Some show up elsewhere in the Solar system, however — some as meteoroids. Many scientists feel that the two moons of Mars are actually 'captured' asteroids.

aurora: light at the North and South Poles caused by the collision of the solar wind with our outer atmosphere.

corona: the thin outer atmosphere of the Sun.

flares: explosions near sunspots that give off great energy.

fusion: the coming together of hydrogen atoms. This produces enormous energy.

granule: one of the cell-like spots on the Sun's surface that disappear after a brief time, usually about eight minutes. An average granule is about 1,000 km across.

gravity: the force that causes objects like the Sun and its planets to be attracted to one another.

helium: a gas formed in the Sun by the fusion of hydrogen atoms.

hydrogen: a colourless, odourless gas that is the simplest and lightest of the elements. The Sun is about three-quarters hydrogen.

neutrinos: very tiny particles produced when hydrogen fuses to helium in the centre of the Sun.

prominences: dark ribbons between sunspots that may occur just before flares become active.

radio telescope: an instrument that uses a radio receiver and antenna to see into space and listen for messages from space.

red giants: huge stars that may be 640 million km across.

Skylab: a satellite carrying humans launched in 1973.

Solar system: the Sun with the planets and all the other bodies, such as the asteroids, that orbit the Sun.

solar wind: tiny particles that travel from the Sun's surface at a speed of 500 km a second.

spectroscope, spectroheliograph, and coronagraph: devices used by scientists to study the Sun.

Sun: our star and provider of the energy that makes life possible on Earth.

sunspot: a dark area on the Sun caused by gases that are cooler and shine less brightly than hot gases.

total solar eclipse: the blocking of the entire body of the Sun by the Moon.

Index

The publishers wish to thank the following for permission to reproduce copyright material: front cover, pp. 8, 16 (lower), 17 (both), 20 (upper right), 24, 26, courtesy of NASA; pp. 4, 16 (upper right), © George East; pp. 5 (all), 9, © Julian Baum 1987; p. 6, © Lynette Cook 1987; pp. 7 (upper right), 14, 15 (lower left), 16 (upper left), 18, 21 (lower), 22 (all), 23 (upper), 25, National Optical Astronomy Observatories; p. 7 (upper left), Defense Nuclear Agency; p. 7 (lower), Brookhaven National Laboratory; pp. 10-11, British Museum, Michael Holford Photographs; pp. 12, 13, Big Bear Solar Observatory; p. 15 (upper), Sacramento Peak Solar Observatory; pp. 15 (lower right), 21 (upper), 28-29, © Sally Bensusen 1987; p. 19 (both upper), © Forrest Baldwin; p. 20 (upper left & lower right), © Richard Hill; p. 19 (lower), © Mark Paternostro 1987; p. 23 (lower), © James Peterson; p. 27, © Mark Maxwell 1987.

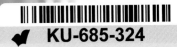

Experiments with ELECTRICITY AND MAGNETISM

TREVOR COOK

W
FRANKLIN WATTS
LONDON•SYDNEY

First published in 2009 by Franklin Watts

Franklin Watts
338 Euston Road
London NW1 3BH

Franklin Watts Australia
Level 17/207 Kent Street, Sydney, NSW 2000

Produced by Arcturus Publishing Limited,
26/27 Bickels Yard, 151–153 Bermondsey Street,
London SE1 3HA

Editor: Alex Woolf
Designers: Sally Henry and Trevor Cook
Consultant: Keith Clayson
Picture Credits: Sally Henry and Trevor Cook

A CIP catalogue record for this book is available
from the British Library.

Dewey Decimal Classification Number: 537

ISBN 978 0 7496 8351 1

Printed in China

Franklin Watts is a division of Hachette Children's Books,
an Hachette Livre UK company.
www.hachettelivre.co.uk

Contents

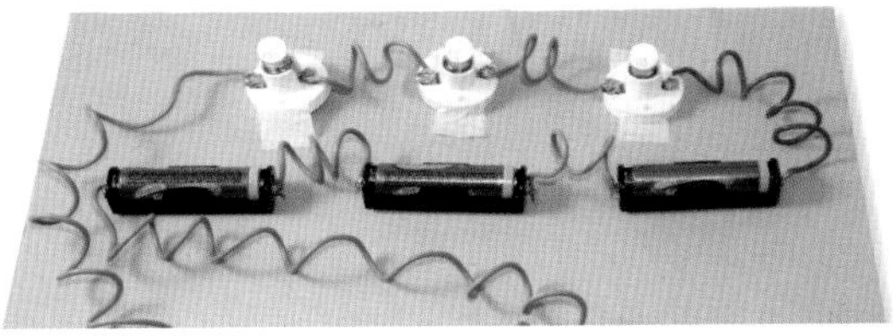

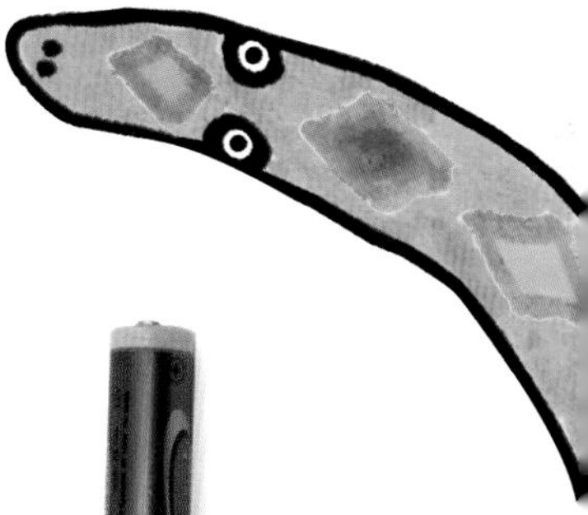

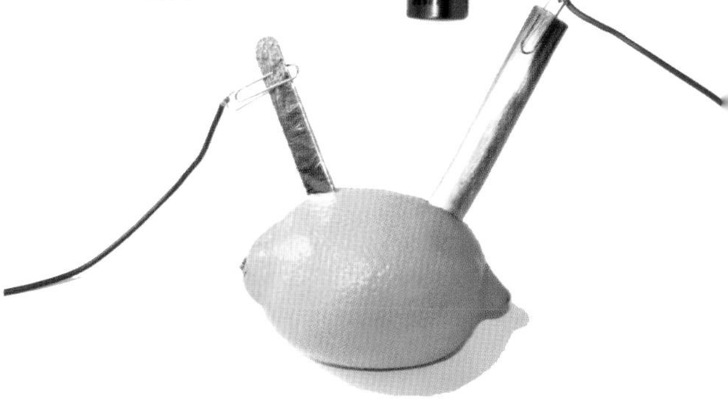

Introduction

From the earliest times, Man has seen and heard the power of electricity.

Now electricity is essential for modern life. Look around your home. Count how many things you can find that work by electricity.

How many of these things need electricity to work?
How many of these things have magnets in them?

brains

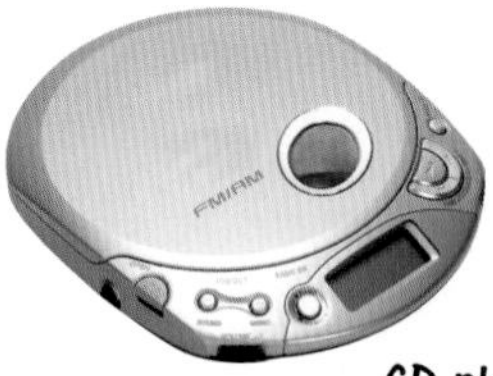

CD player

drill

toy train

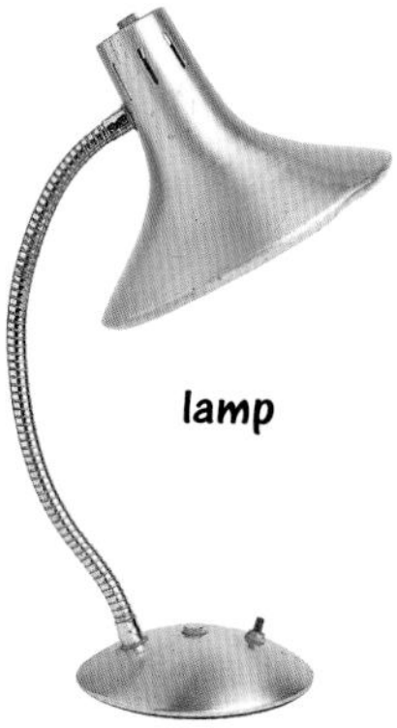

lamp

radio

mobile phone

lemon

Answers: They all need electricity to work except the lemon. We'll be using the lemon to make electricity later on in the book.

Anything that has an electric motor or a loudspeaker has magnets. So there are no magnets in the lamp (or the lemon!). The toy train has magnetic couplings – we'll need them on page 27.

We make electricity from other forms of energy. We can burn fuel, such as coal or oil, or use natural forces such as wind or water.

Electricity is carried to where it is needed by metal cables. The cables are held up on big towers called pylons. The thicker the cables, the more electricity they can carry.

In our home, we connect things to this supply of electricity through plugs and sockets, and the electricity flows through smaller wires.

In our experiments we're going to use batteries. Later on, we'll make our own electricity (see page 18).

Long ago, magnetism was thought to be a form of magic. Early navigators, such as the Vikings, used special pieces of magnetic rock, called 'lodestone', as simple compasses to help them find their way in strange seas.

Looking at magnets starts on page 22. You will need a compass when you get to page 26.

a piece of lodestone

Some technical or unusual words, shown in *italic* type, are explained in the glossary on page 31.

Materials and tools

You should easily find many things that you need for our experiments around the home.

20 minutes

This tells you about how long a project could take.

This symbol means you might need adult help.

Wire The kind of wire found inside power cords of domestic appliances is generally ideal. Ask an adult to help you by taking off the outer covering. Inside you'll find two or three coloured wires. If you need stiffer wire, as in the coil experiment on page 30, use the single conductor wire from lighting cable. Ask an electrician for offcuts!

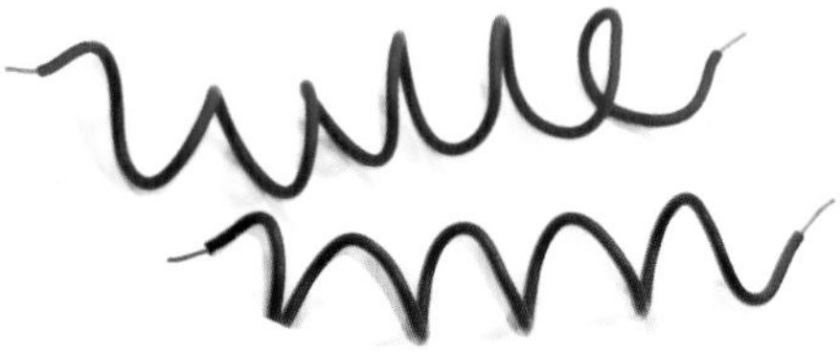

Batteries We've used a size that's called AA in the UK. It's a very common size and you'll find them used in lots of things around the home.

Tape We use sticky tape to hold things in position. Masking tape or clear parcel tape will do.

Bulbs Torch bulbs rated between 1.5 and 4.5 volts with an MES fitting are ideal.

Bulb holder You need one of these for each bulb you use. Buy them at the same time as your bulbs.

Circuit board This can be made of anything that you can easily attach components to. We've used a piece of softboard.

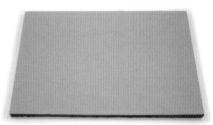

Glue stick is mostly used for sticking paper to paper.

Universal glue is a rubbery stuff that sticks most things to most other things!

Buzzer Find one that works on low voltages – around 2–3 volts.

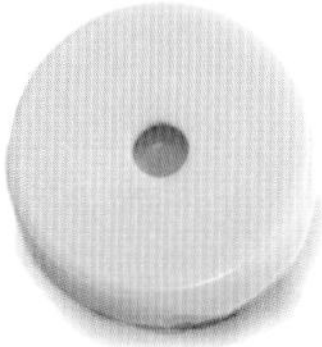

Magnets Most of our magnetism experiments use bar magnets, but horseshoe magnets work just as well.

Iron filings These are usually sold in a clear plastic container. You can see the effects of magnetism without opening it.

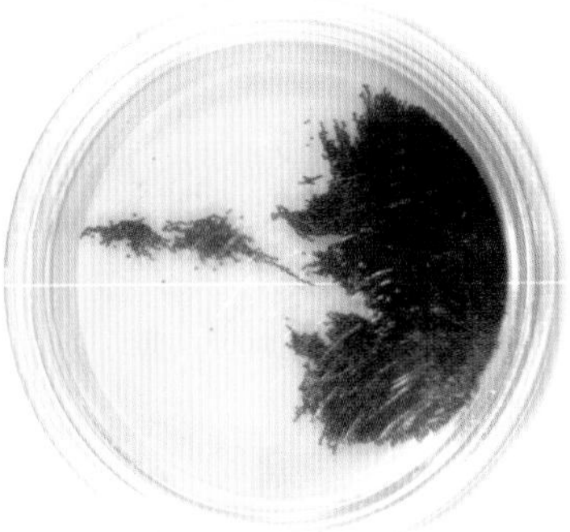

Compass The smallest toy compass is great for these experiments.

Lodestone You can find pieces in museum shops or on the Internet.

Copper tubing is an excellent source of copper. Get an adult to ask their friendly plumber for offcuts – they're often thrown away!

Friends can help
Do the experiments with your friends!

Digital LED clock or calculator Sold in supermarkets or 'pound stores', they are often much cheaper than a pound! The great thing is that they don't need much electricity to make them go. You can get them to work on tiny currents.

Wire stripper In the experiments you'll always need to have the metal conductor exposed at the end of the wires. This hand tool is used to remove insulation. You might have one in your household tool kit.
Get an adult to help you do this!

Scissors Use safe scissors that you can keep for all your experiments. Keep them away from young children.

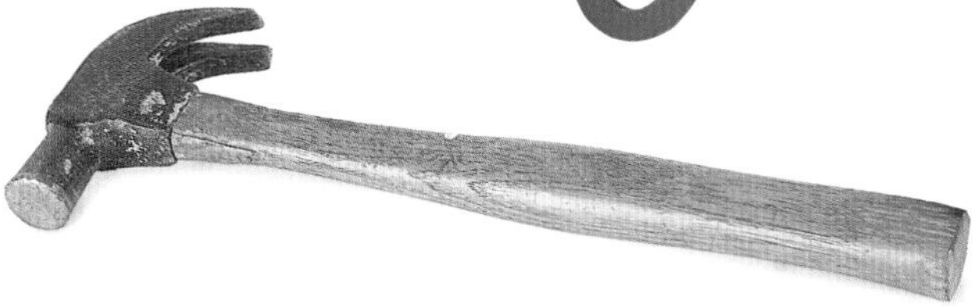

Hammer Most homes have a hammer somewhere. Take care when you use it and put it away when you've finished!

Making a circuit

20 minutes

Electricity is carried in a *circuit*. The power lines on page 5 and the power cords on page 6 are all parts of circuits.

You will need:

- insulated wire
- *MES* bulb and bulb holder,
- sticky tape
- *battery*
- board
- scissors
- paper clips
- drawing pins

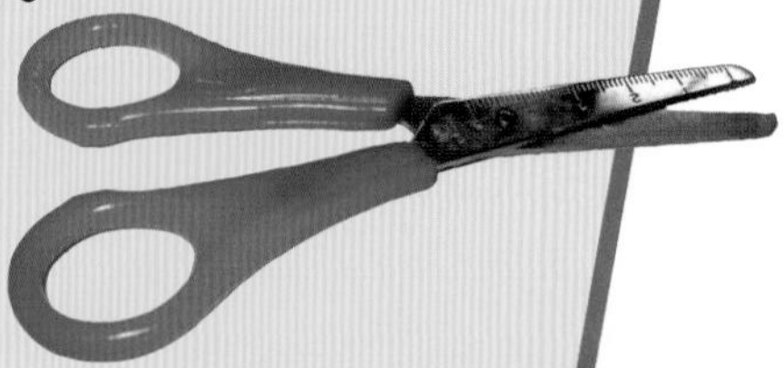

The plan

We are going to make our own circuit.

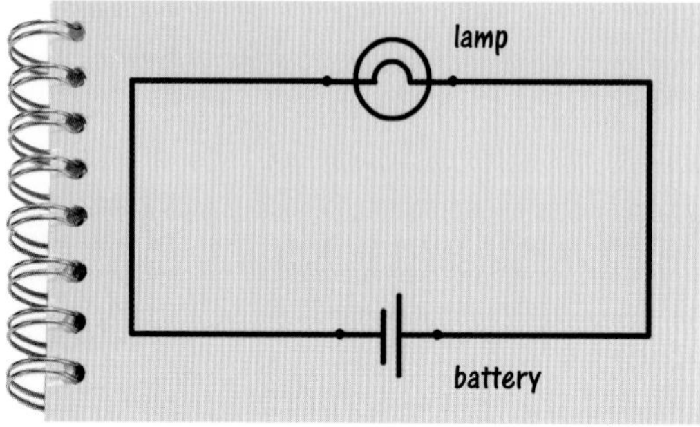

Jargon Buster

A **lamp** is made up of a bulb and a bulb holder.

What to do:

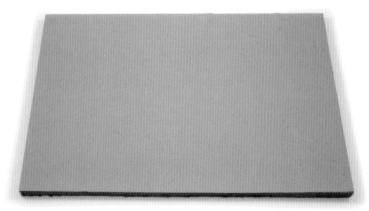

1 We need a piece of board to build our circuit on. This is a piece of softboard. You could use wood or plywood. Make it about 300 x 200 mm (12 x 8 in).

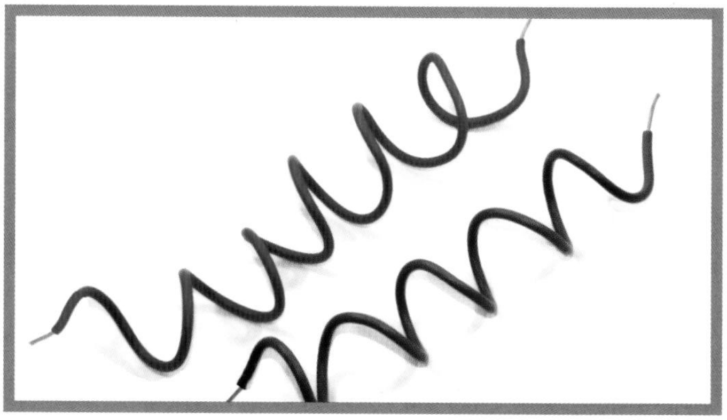

2 Prepare your wire by stripping the coloured insulation from both ends.

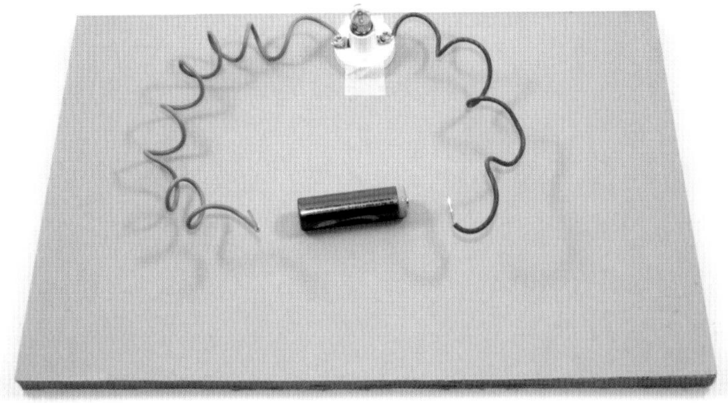

3 We've fixed the lamp to the board with some sticky tape to make things tidier.

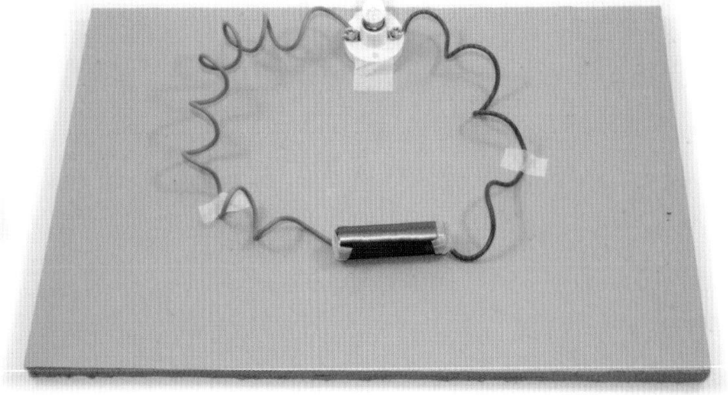

4 Fix one end of each wire to the lamp and the other ends to the battery using sticky tape.

What's going on?

The lamp comes on because we've made a continuous circuit connecting the battery and lamp.

What else can you do?

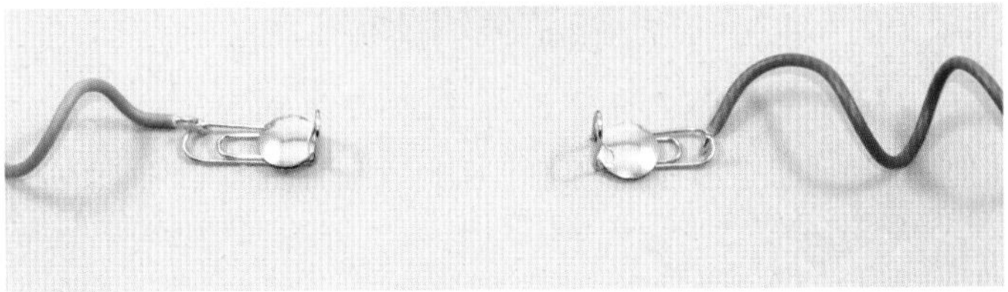

Use two paper clips (not plastic coated) and two drawing pins to make a battery holder like this.

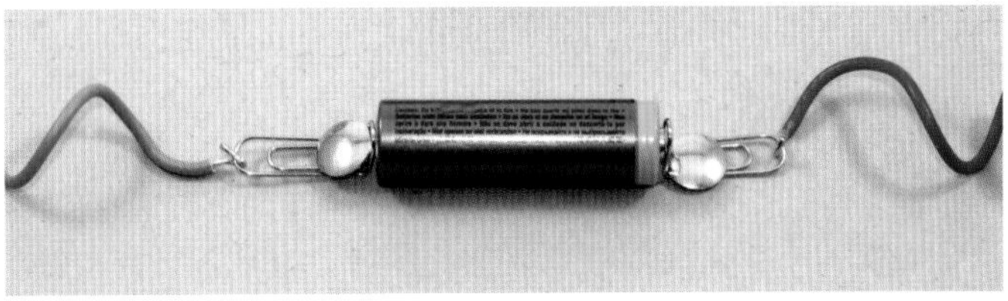

The battery should be held firmly in place between the paper clips.

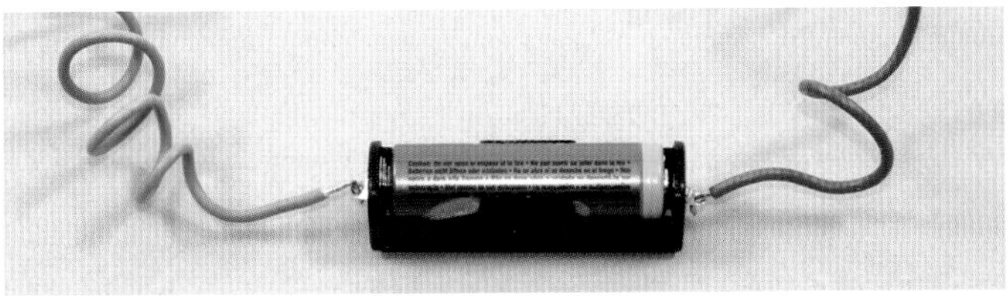

Alternatively, you can use a battery holder to give a reliable fixing point for the wires.

Jargon Buster

Completing the circuit means allowing the current to flow.

Conductors and insulators

Which materials can electricity pass through? Those which allow electricity to pass through are called *conductors*. Those that don't are called *insulators*.

35 minutes

The plan

We take the circuit we built on pages 8 and 9 and use it to find out whether materials are conductors or insulators.

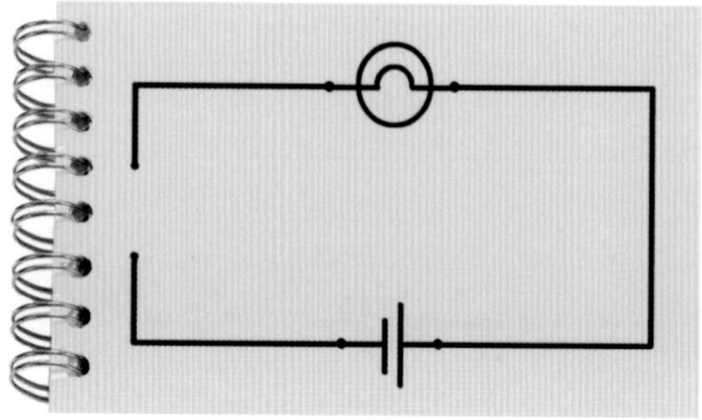

You will need:

- the circuit from page 9
- a selection of small objects – metallic and non-metallic such as:
  ball-point pen
  plastic comb
  nail
  flower
  string
  coin

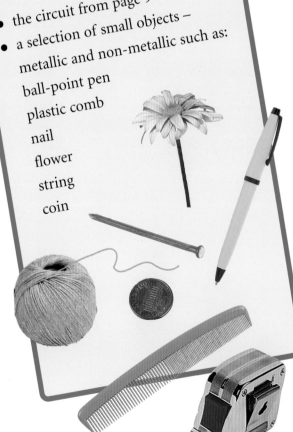

What to do:

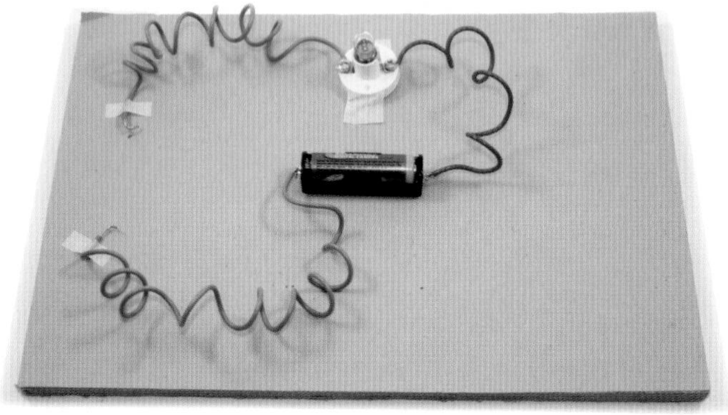

1 Add a new wire to the circuit we made on page 9. We've decided to use a battery holder this time.

2 We are going to use the ends of the wire to test different materials.

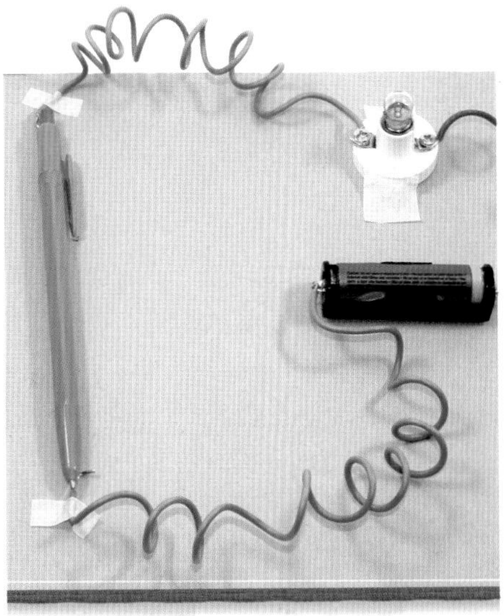

3 A plastic pen doesn't complete the circuit.

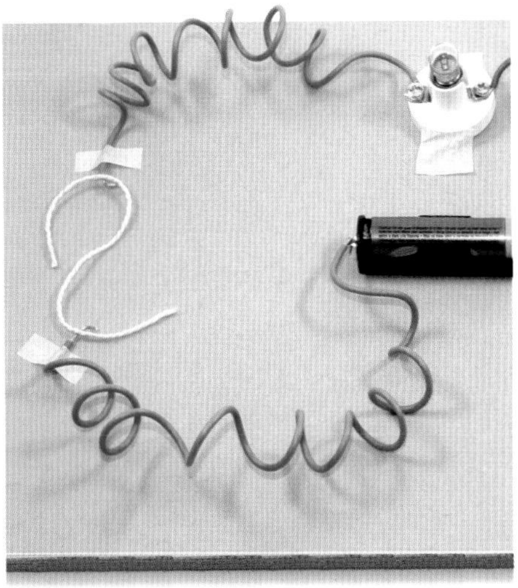

4 Neither does the string.

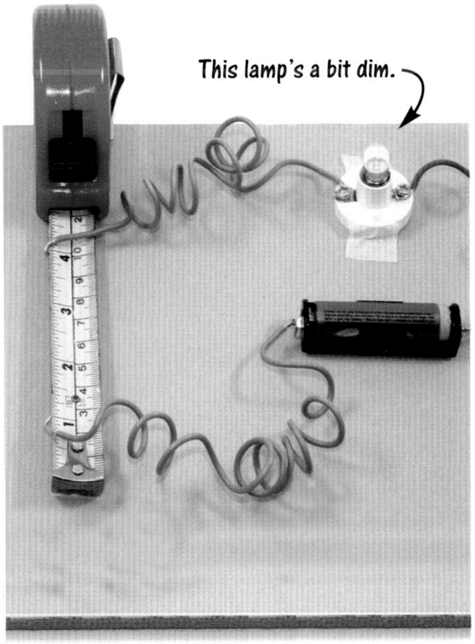

5 The paint on the tape measure is resisting the current.

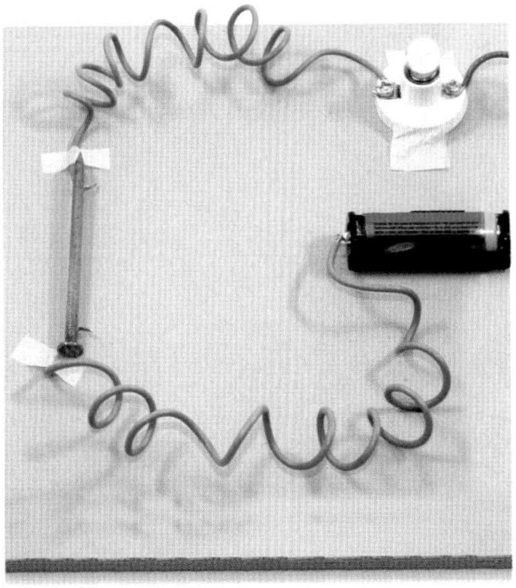

6 This nail is made of iron.

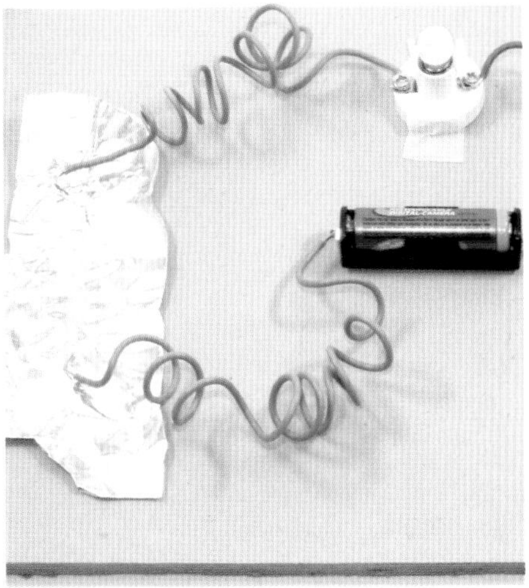

7 Here's a piece of kitchen foil.

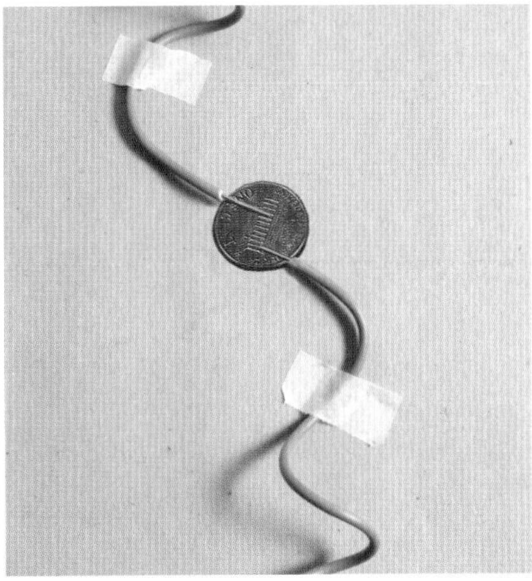

8 Will this coin complete the circuit? What about the flower?

What's going on?

Most conductors are metal. We use insulators such as plastics to stop electricity going where we don't want it to go.

What else can you do?

Look at these tools. Why do you think they've got thick rubbery handles?

Switches

30 minutes

We've made a circuit that lights lamps but we probably don't want it to be on all the time.

You will need:

- the circuit we made in the previous pages
- 2 drawing pins
- a paper clip

The plan

Let's make a simple switch to turn the lamp on and off.

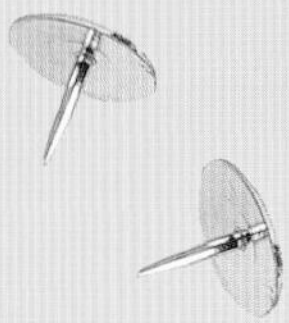

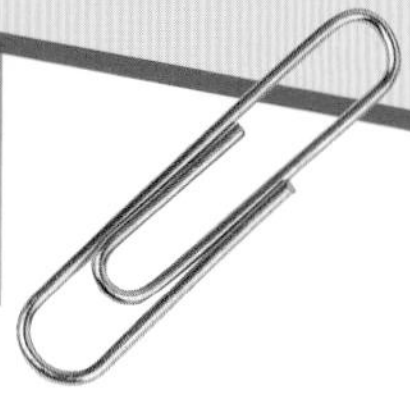

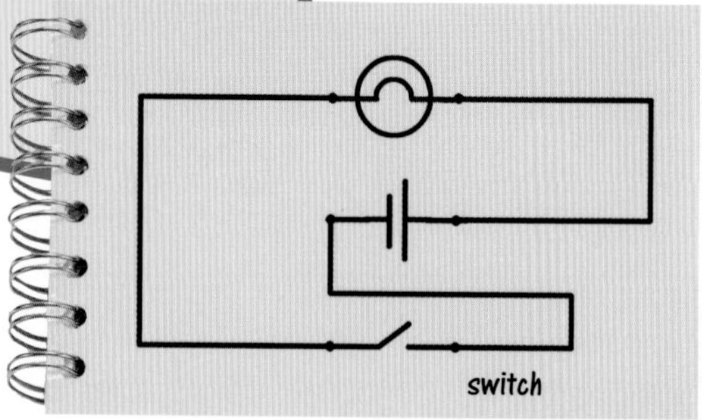

What to do:

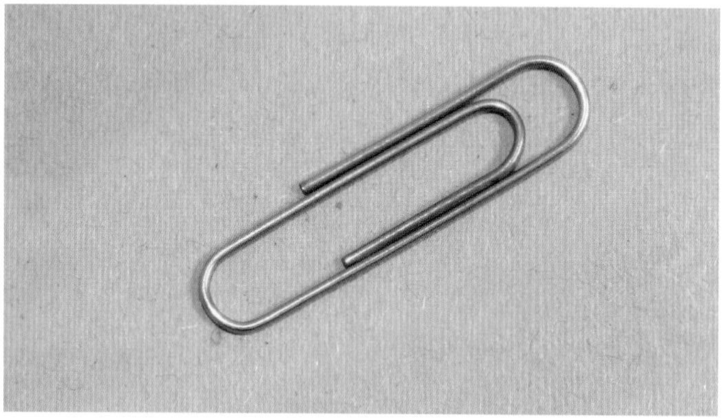

1 Your paper clip must be made of metal and not painted or coated with plastic.

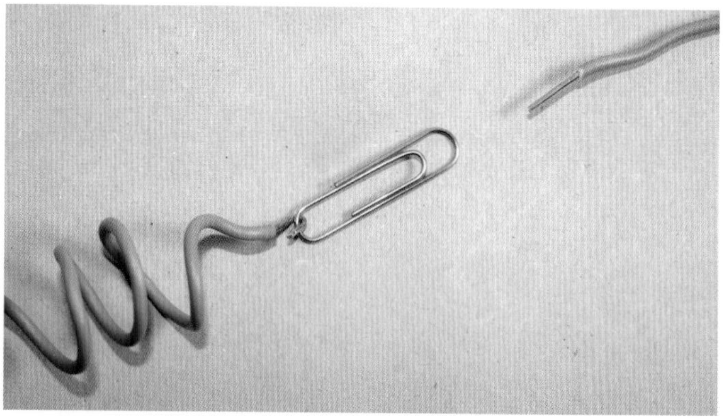

2 Test the paper clip as a conductor by the method we used in the last experiment.

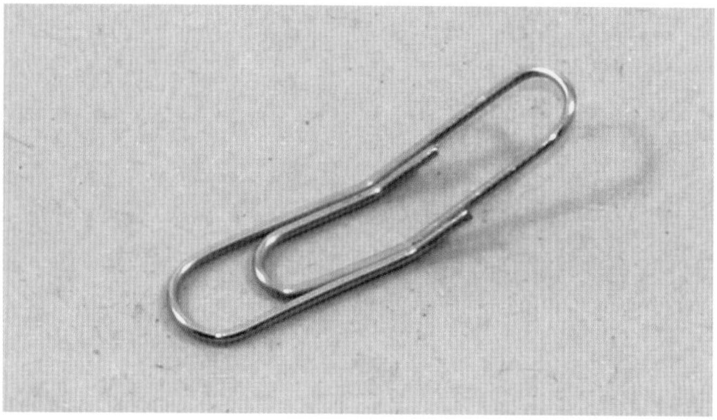

3 Bend the paper clip a little in the middle.

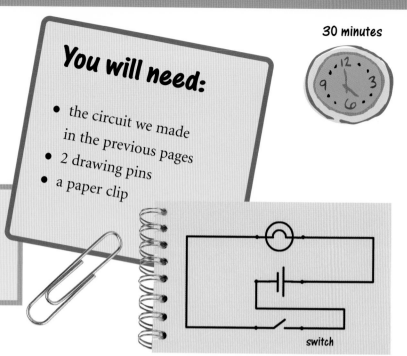

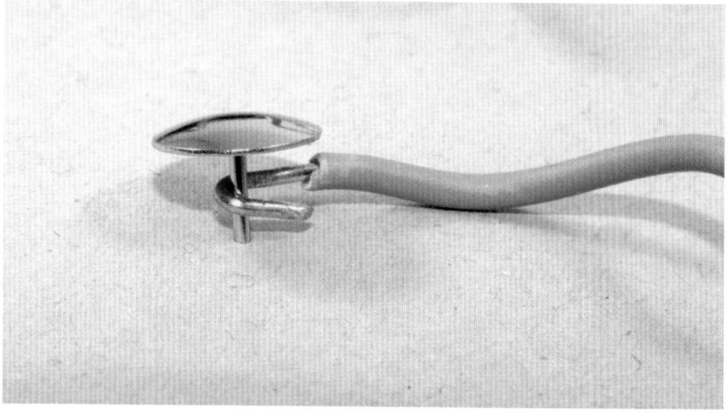

4 Bend the bare wire end of one of the wires round a drawing pin and press it into the softboard.

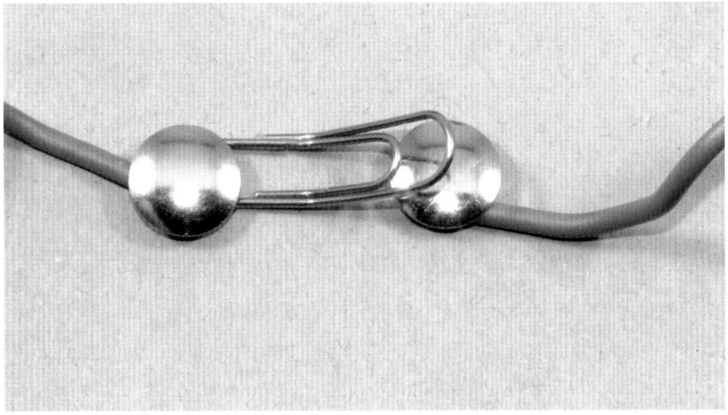

5 The other drawing pin holds the other wire and the paper clip in place.

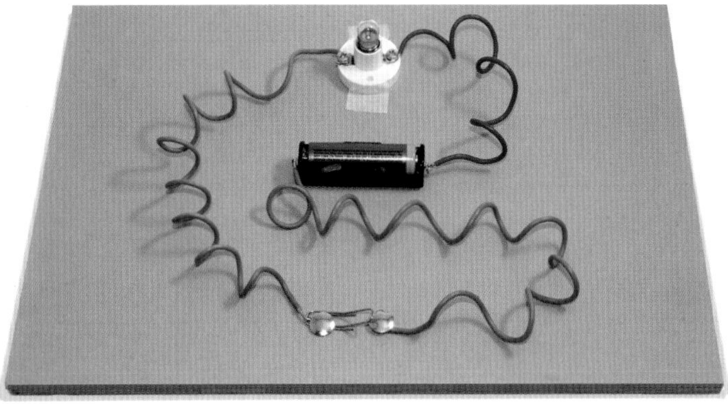

6 Here's the switch in the circuit.

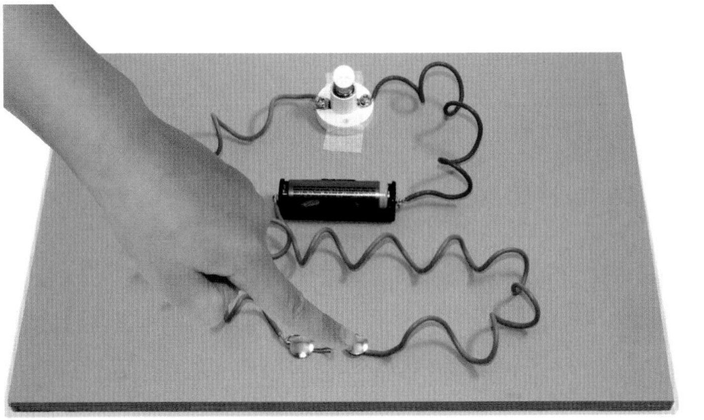

7 Press the switch to turn the lamp on!

What's going on?

Current flows when there's no break in the circuit.

Jargon Buster

Closing the switch means completing the circuit and allowing the current to flow.

What else can you do?

We made a switch that has to be held down to keep the switch closed. You can use the same components to make a switch that stays closed.

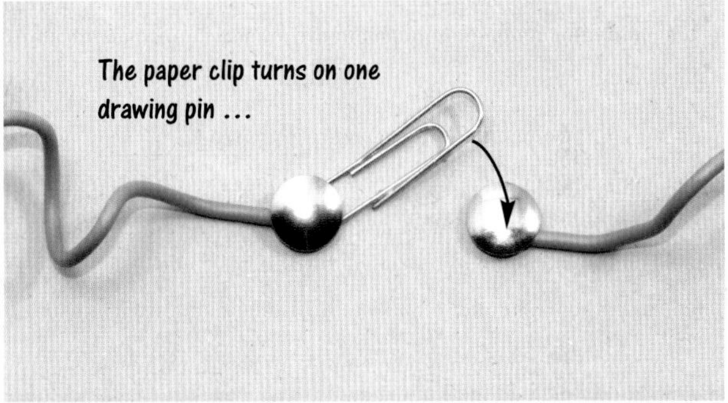

The paper clip turns on one drawing pin ...

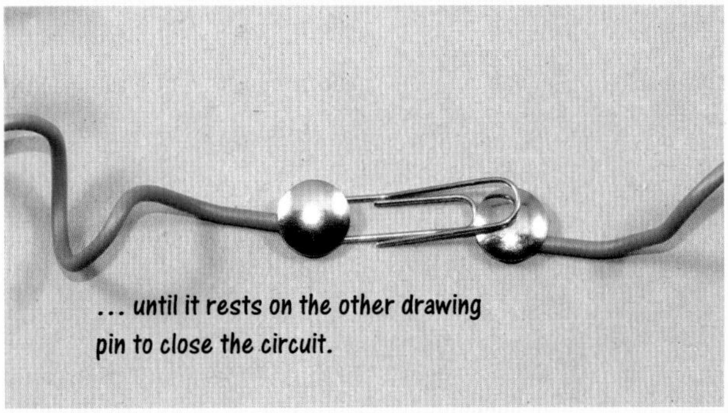

... until it rests on the other drawing pin to close the circuit.

More light!

40 minutes

What happens when we want more light? Do we make more circuits like the one on the last page, or can we just add more lamps to the circuit? Let's find out!

The plan

We are going to connect more bulbs to the circuit.

You will need:

- the circuit from the last experiment
- 2 more bulbs and lamp holders
- 2 short lengths of wire with insulation stripped from the ends

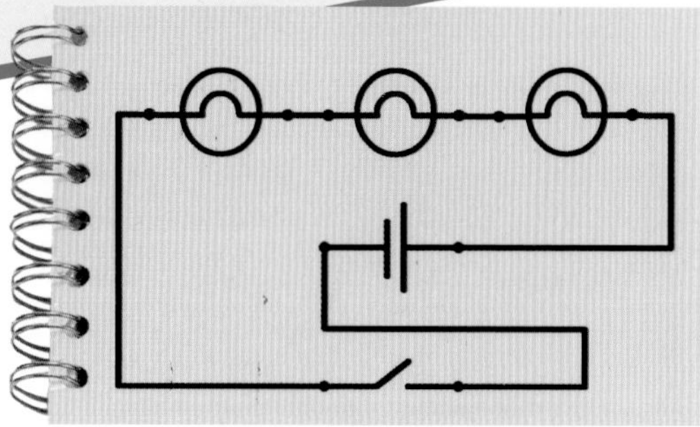

Experiment 1

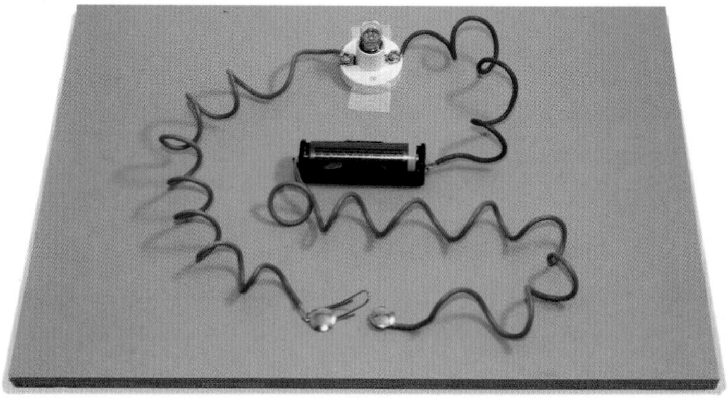

1 Take the circuit we made last time. Make sure the switch is turned off.

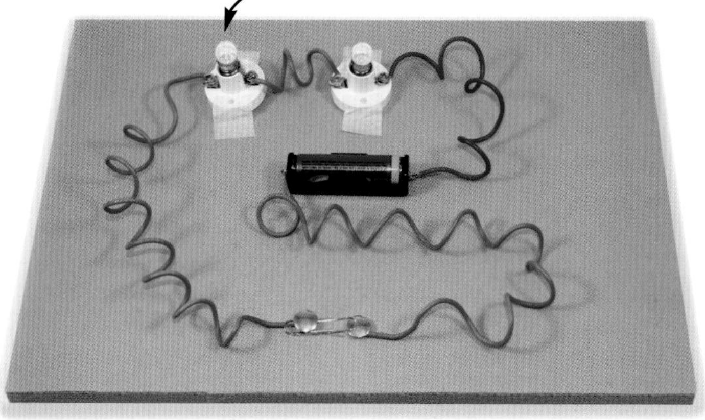

2 Connect another lamp in the circuit next to the first one. Switch on the current.

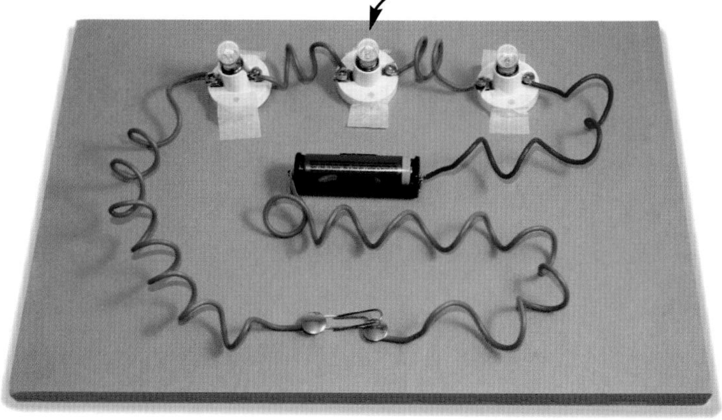

3 Switch off and connect another lamp to the circuit to make three. Switch on again.

What's going on?

We've connected the bulbs together in the circuit like a daisy chain. This is called *in series*. Every bulb we add to the circuit increases the energy required for the electricity to flow.

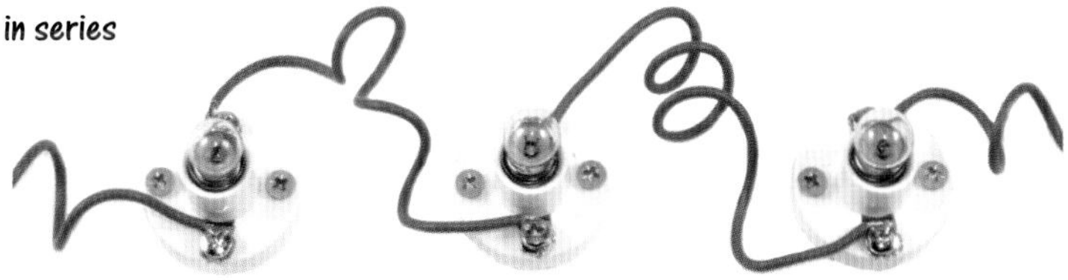

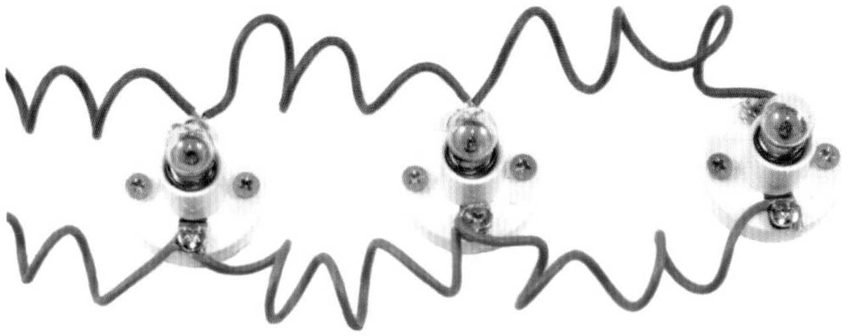

Experiment 2

There's another way to use electricity in a circuit, *in parallel*. Let's see what difference it makes to the result.

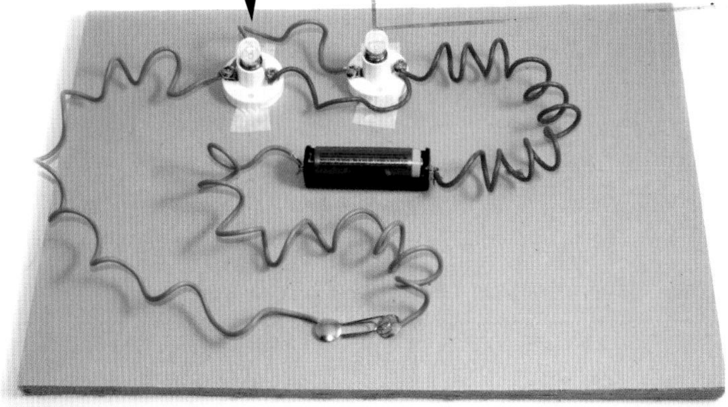

1 Start as in Step 1, page 14. Connect one more lamp, using two more wires. Switch on.

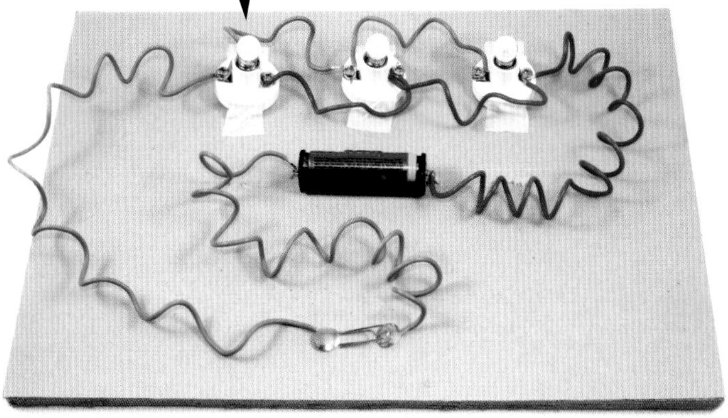

2 Switch off and connect a third lamp with two more wires. Switch on again.

What's going on?

This time we've connected the lamps in parallel. Each bulb in the circuit gets the right amount of electricity to make it work. The battery might not last for long running three bulbs, though.

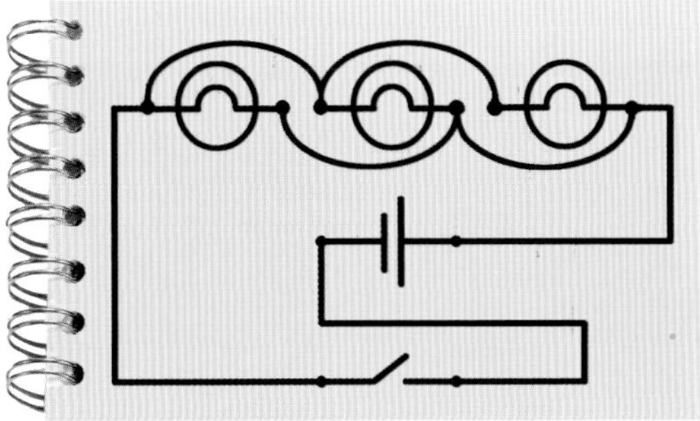

What else can you do?

We wanted more light – it seems we'll need more power! Let's look at batteries in the next section.

Jargon Buster

A **terminal** is the means of connecting wires to devices like batteries or lamps.

Power up!

35 minutes

How do we add more power to the circuit? Is there a clue in looking at the different ways the lamps worked in the circuit?

You will need:

- the circuit from the last experiment
- 2 drawing pins, a paper clip
- 4 wires

The plan

Let's try connecting more batteries to the circuit in different ways.

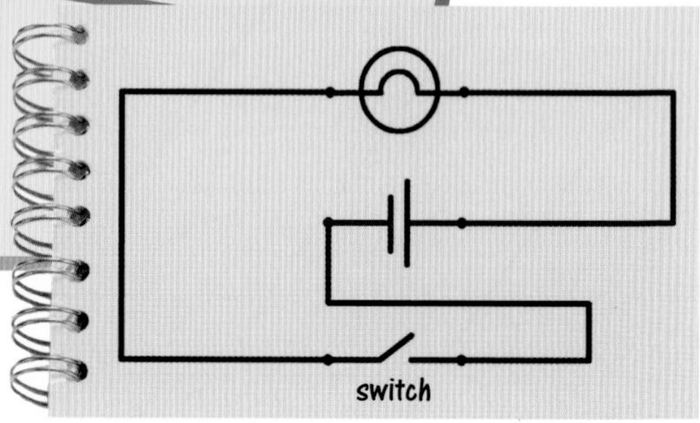

What to do:

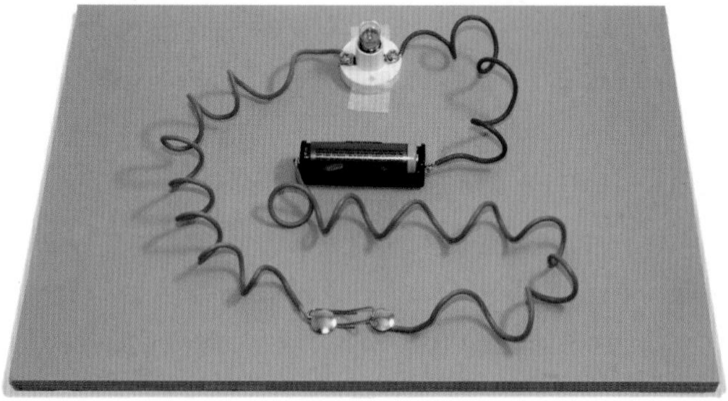

1 Start with the circuit as in picture 6, page 13.

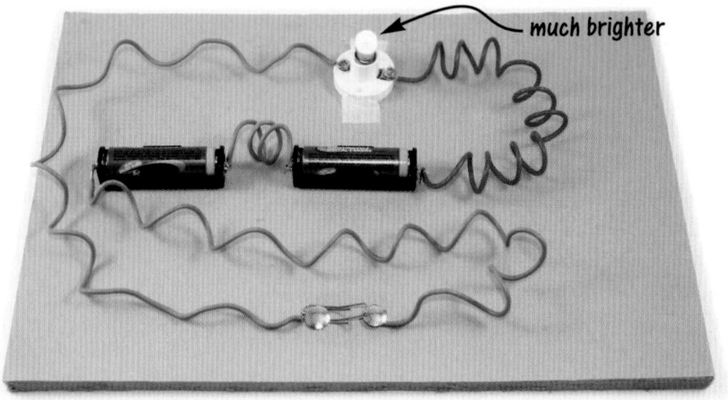

2 Connect a second battery into the circuit. Switch on.

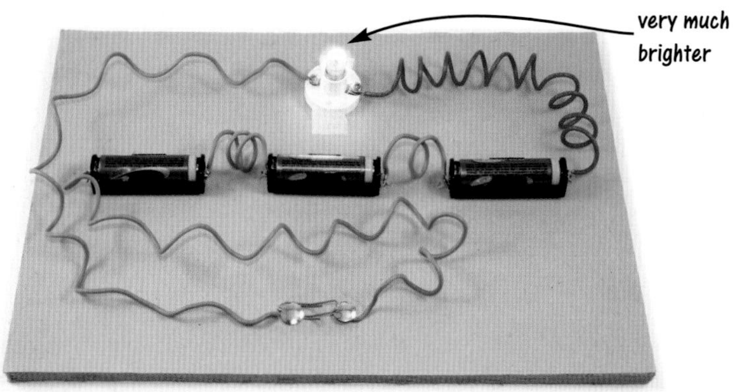

3 Add a third battery to the circuit. The lamp is much too bright now. It might burn out!

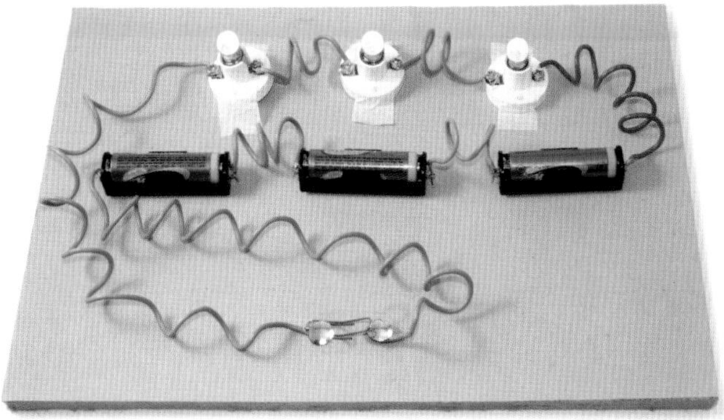

4 Try adding more lamps in series.

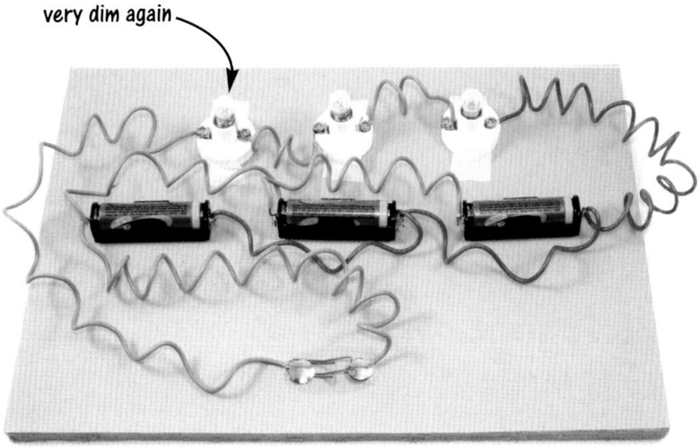

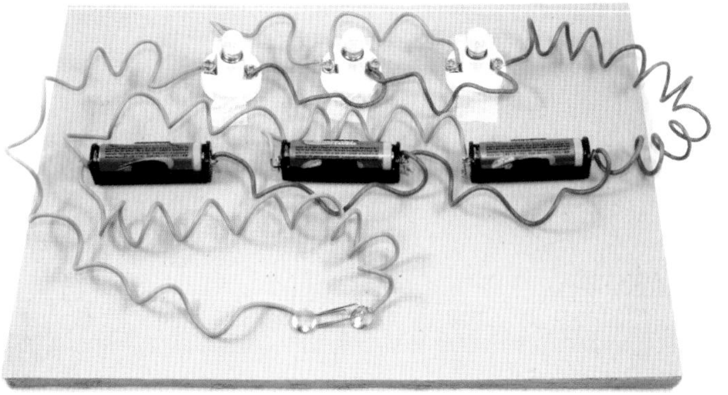

5 Now connect the batteries in parallel, as you did with your lamps on page 15.

6 Now connect together both the lamps and the batteries in parallel.

What's going on?

Adding more batteries makes one lamp burn brighter, but it will soon burn out. Connecting batteries and more lamps in parallel produces more light without burn-outs.

What else can you do?

Wire components together partly in series, partly in parallel. Try combinations and predict the result.

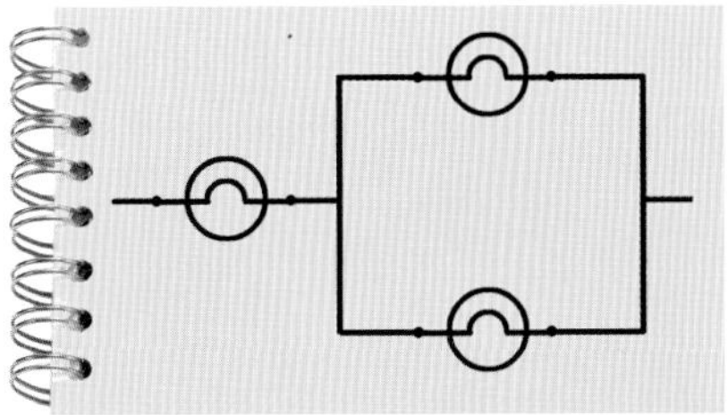

three lamps: one in series, two in parallel

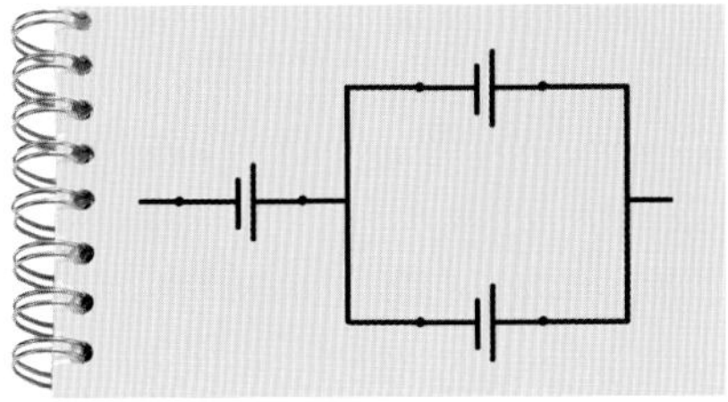

three batteries: one in series, two in parallel

Jargon Buster

The measure of energy in an electric circuit is the **volt**. The small batteries in our experiments produce about 1.5 volts.

The lemon battery

40 minutes

When you've got tired of buying fresh batteries for your experiments, here's a way of making your own. The trouble is, you may have to buy some lemons instead!

The plan

We are going to produce electricity and power a device using fresh fruit!

You will need:

- three ice lolly sticks
- aluminium kitchen foil
- 3 lemons
- 8 paper clips
- 3 pieces of copper tube about 100 mm (4 in) long
- insulated wire
- device such as an old clock or calculator with an *LCD* display
- small knife

What to do:

1 Get an adult to cut a square hole and a slot in each lemon with a small knife.

2 Wrap the lolly sticks with kitchen foil and push one into the slot of each lemon.

Jargon Buster

Close the circuit means the same as **switch on** and **break the circuit** the same as **switch off.**

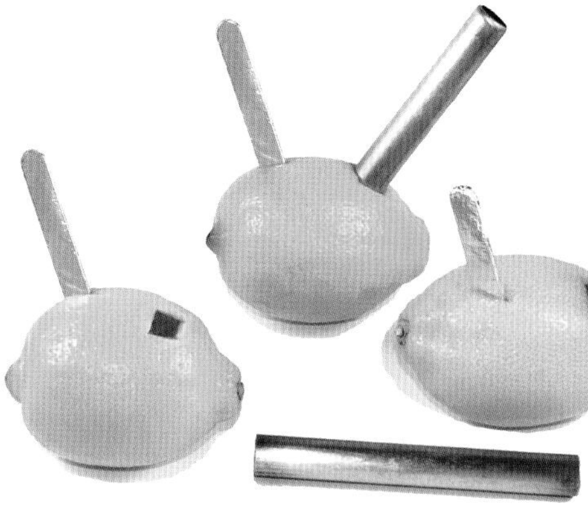

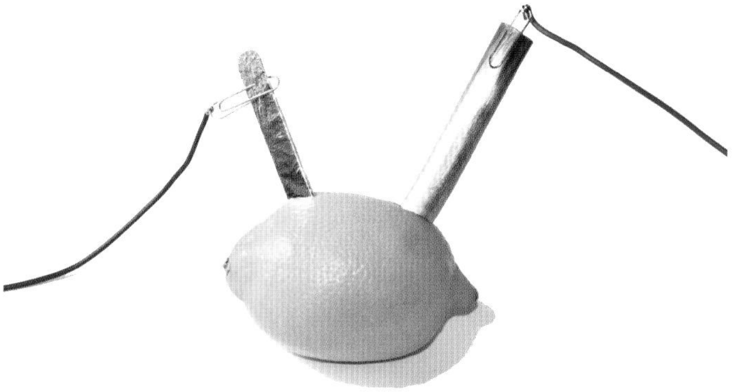

3 Push one piece of copper tube into each lemon.

4 Use paper clips to attach the wires.

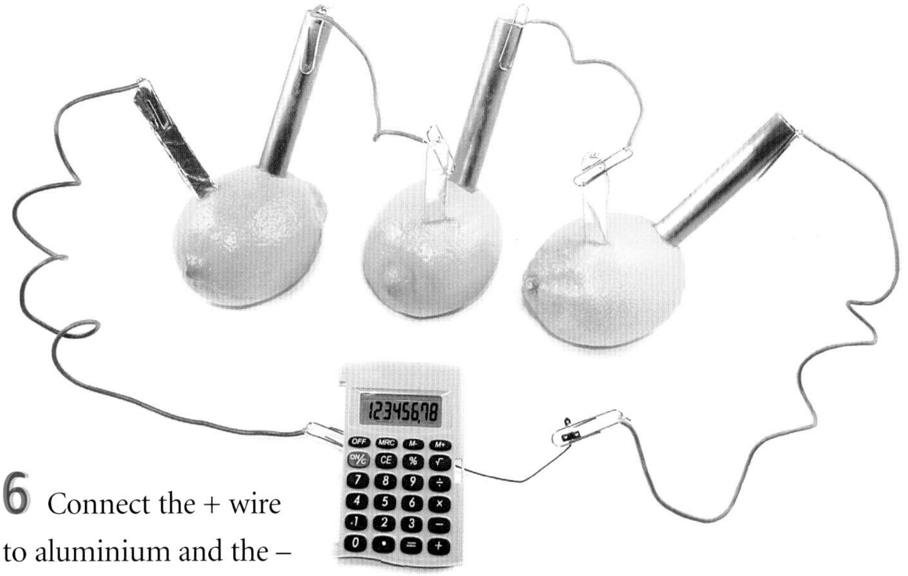

5 Open your display device to remove the battery and reveal the terminals. This calculator has a red wire marked '+' and a black wire marked '–'.

6 Connect the + wire to aluminium and the – wire to copper. In between, make sure copper connects to aluminium.

What's going on?

If we've made all the right connections, after a few minutes we should see the display come on. (If there's a switch, make sure it's on!)

Our lemon battery is producing a charge by having two different metals (aluminium and copper) in an acid liquid (the juice of the lemon). A chemical reaction takes place which also produces an electrical charge. The electricity is conducted through the lemon juice, into the metal and on into the circuit.

What else can you do?

Try different fruits and vegetables!

Jargon Buster

+ means **positive** – means **negative**
Current in a circuit flows from the terminal marked positive to the one marked negative.

Warning~this page is alarmed!

Now we know how to make a circuit with a battery, lamp and switch, it's time to put our knowledge to good use!

35 minutes

The plan

We are going to make a simple alarm system. It's meant to be operated by an intruder stepping on a special switch, called a pressure mat.

You will need:

- two thin sheets of card roughly 250 x 200 mm (10 x 8 in), bigger if you like
- two sheets of kitchen foil – the same area as the cardboard
- thin sponge sheet (sold in craft shops)
- two paper clips
- two long pieces of wire, with stripped ends
- the circuit from page 13
- glue stick, universal glue
- small *buzzer*

What to do:

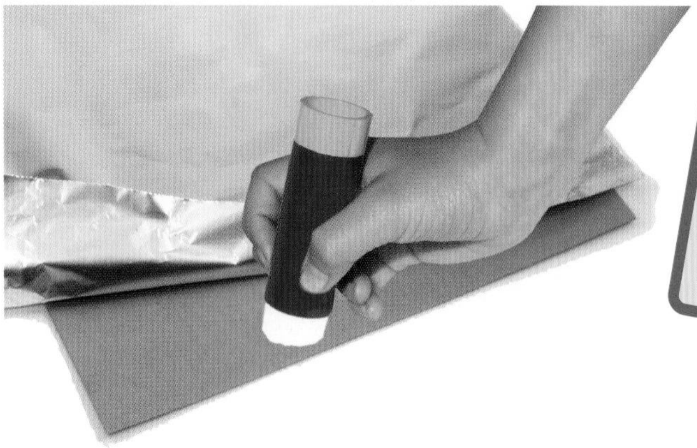

1 Stick foil to both sheets of card.

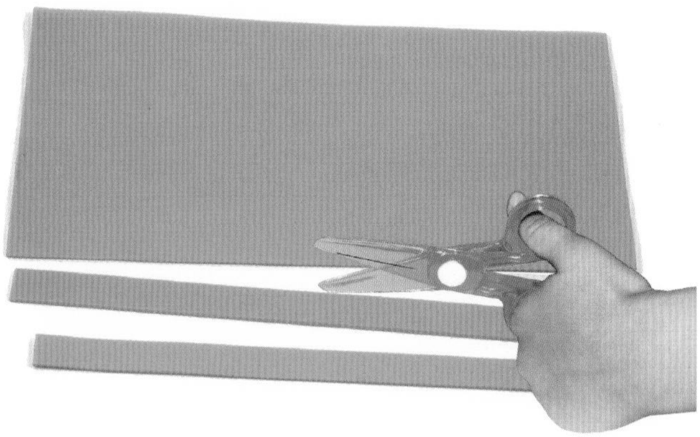

2 Cut the sponge into strips 12 mm (0.5 in) wide.

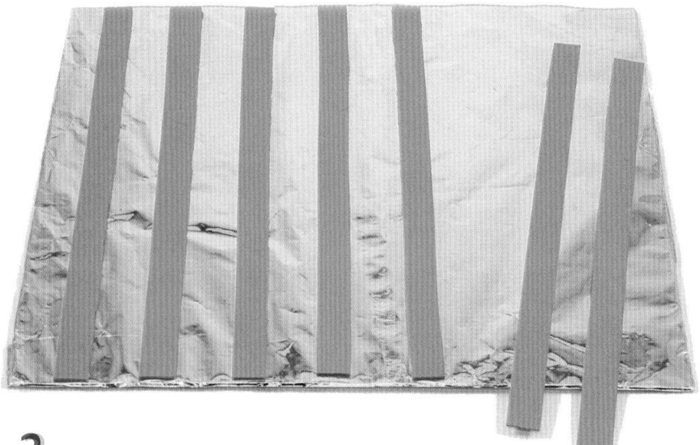

3 Stick the sponge strips on one foil-covered sheet with a glue stick.

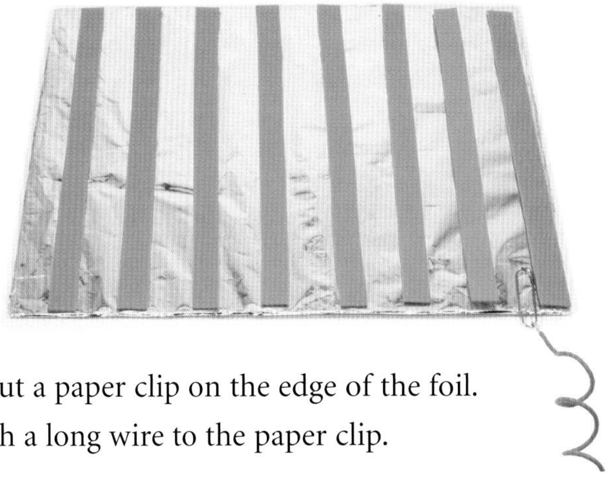

4 Put a paper clip on the edge of the foil. Attach a long wire to the paper clip.

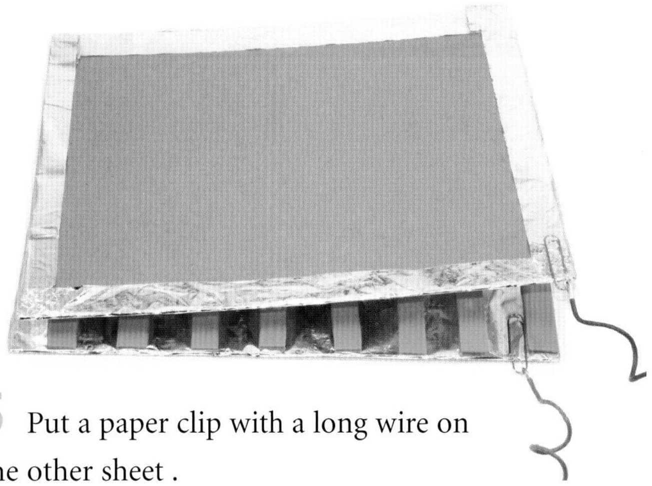

5 Put a paper clip with a long wire on the other sheet .

6 Use sticky tape to join the two sheets together, foil side inwards. Make sure the paper clips and bare wires can't touch accidentally. This is your new switch.

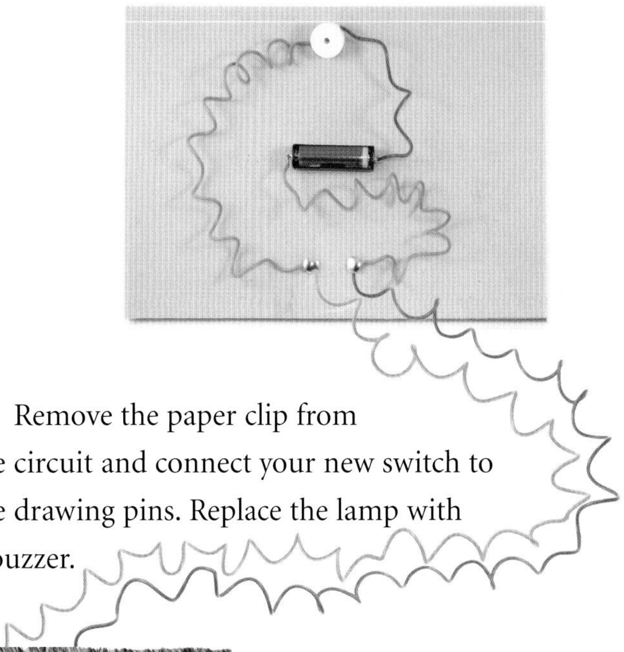

7 Remove the paper clip from the circuit and connect your new switch to the drawing pins. Replace the lamp with a buzzer.

8 We've put the new switch under a mat.

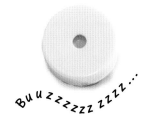

What's going on?

The weight of someone treading on the pad will complete the circuit and set off the alarm.

What else can you do?

You can make a similar switch that closes when a weight is taken off it.

Attractive stuff

15 minutes

You will need:

- at least one magnet – or as many kinds of magnet you can get.
- *iron filings*
- some objects to test for magnetism, including some made of metal
- a hammer and a piece of scrap wood

There's a close connection between electricity and another natural force – *magnetism.* Before we find out more about this connection, we need to look at *magnets,* what they are and how they are made.

The plan

We're going to find out more about the force of magnetism and what it can do.

Experiment 1

1 Take a magnet and find out which kind of thing is attracted to it.

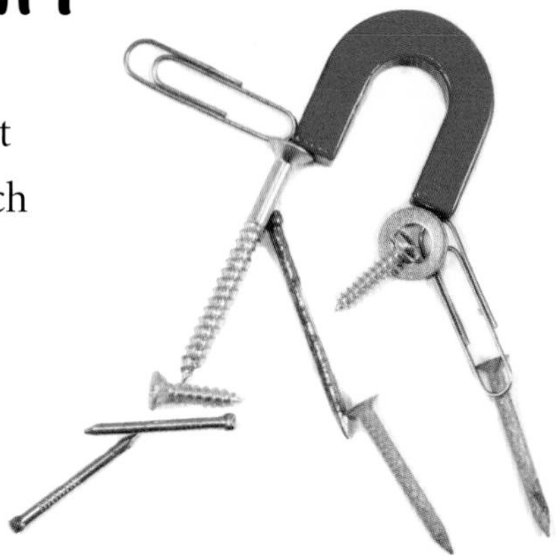

2 The objects on the right are attracted to the magnet, those on the left are not.

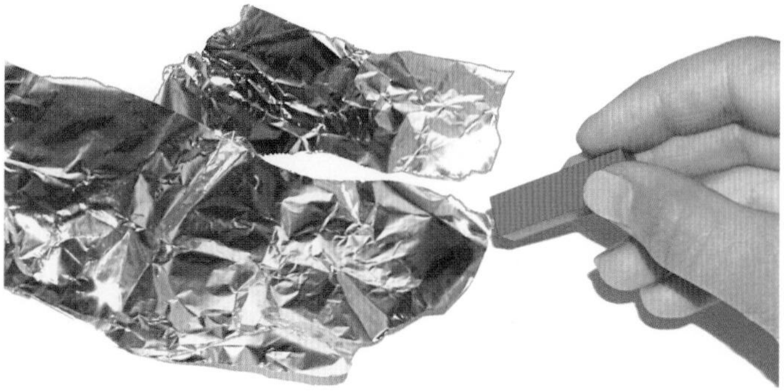

3 It seems that all the things that the magnet will pick up are metal. But not all metal things are magnetic. Try the magnet with some kitchen foil (aluminium).

Jargon Buster

A **permanent** magnet means one that does not lose its magnetism after a short time.

4 You can use iron filings to see that the effect is strongest nearest to the magnet, and that a pattern forms between one end and the other.

What's going on?

All things that are magnetic contain iron.

Experiment 2

You can use a magnet to make a new one.

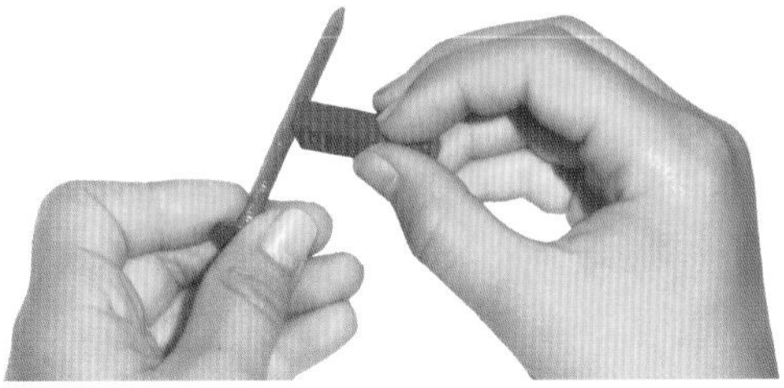

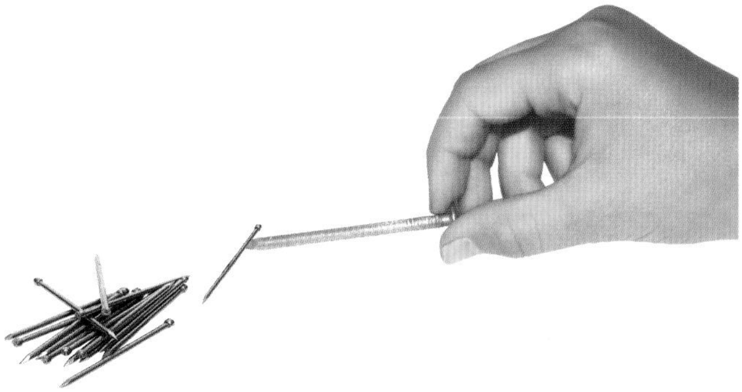

1 Take a nail and stroke it lengthways with one end of the magnet, lifting it away at the end, always using the same end of the magnet.

2 The new magnet won't be as strong as the one that made it, but it can still pick things up!

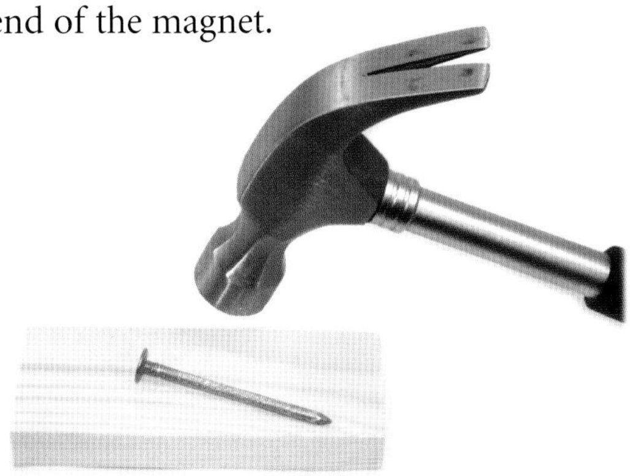

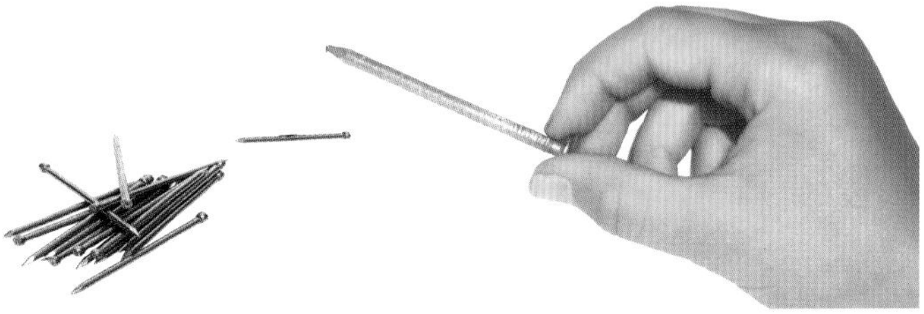

3 Put the magnetised nail on a firm surface and tap it with a hammer along its length. Try not to bend it!

4 We have destroyed the magnetism in the nail.

What's going on?

Nails are made of iron in which the *molecules* are like little magnets arranged randomly. The effect of all the little magnets is to cancel out each other's magnetism. A magnet works because its molecules are all pointing the same way. Stroking a piece of iron (the nail) with a magnet gradually lines up the molecules, magnetising it.

Hitting the nail with a hammer jars the molecules back into their random arrangement, destroying the magnetic effect.

30 minutes

Invisible forces

Let's look a little more closely at what magnetism can do.

The plan

We are going to look at the ability of magnetism to pass through materials.

You will need:

- two magnets
- a sheet of thin card A4 (8.25 x 11.75 ins)
- marker pen
- two paper clips (different colours would be best)
- a plain glass jar with a plastic lid, clear sides and no labels
- paper, coloured pencils or markers, scissors, sticky tape
- a clean, flat baking tray (check that a magnet will stick to it)

Experiment 1

1 Copy the maze onto A4 size card. You and a friend will each need a magnet and paper clip.

2 Starting at opposite ends, you both guide your 'man' (the paper clip) through the maze using magnets under the card. Each of you chooses an entrance and aims for the exit on the other side. When you've finished, try playing the game again, but this time with the card on a metal baking tray. Will the game still work?

Experiment 2

1 Do the Magic Snake trick and baffle your friends! Copy the snake onto paper. Make it a little smaller if necessary, so that it fits in the bottom of the glass jar. Colour and cut out the snake.

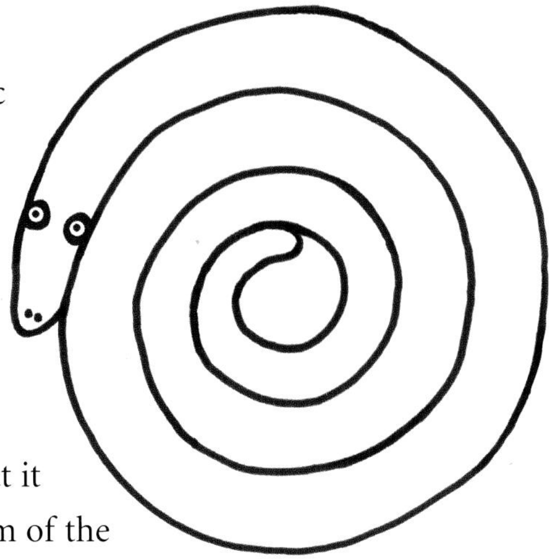

2 Put a paper clip on the snake's head.

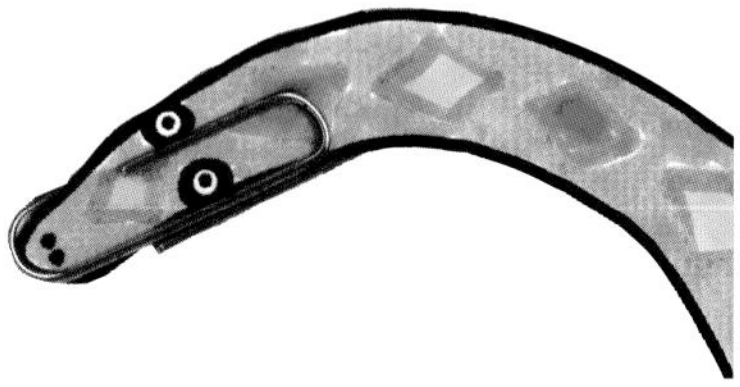

3 Stick the tip of the tail to the bottom of the jar.

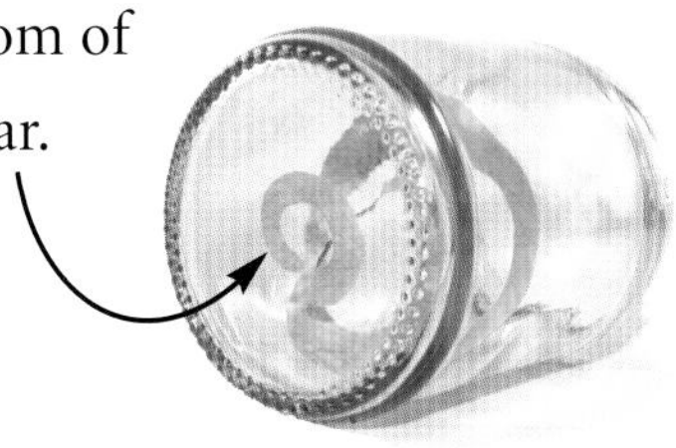

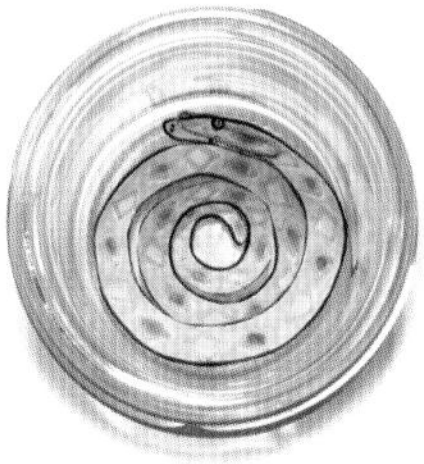

4 Secretly hold a magnet in the palm of your hand as you gently turn the jar upside down and back again.

5 The snake stays up!

6 Take your hand away (with the magnet) and the snake falls down.

What's going on?

In Experiment 1, magnetism passes through the card easily, but not through metal.

In Experiment 2, the snake trick reminds us that just because we can't see something (magnetism), it doesn't mean there's nothing there.

Jargon Buster

A **magnetic field** is the space around a magnet in which magnetism can be detected.

North and south

25 minutes

Magnets are often marked 'N' and 'S' at the ends. We call these *poles*, but what does this mean?

The plan

We're going to see how magnets behave together and find out how to tell which pole is which.

You will need:

- 2 bar magnets
- a small compass
- paper and pencil
- some thread
- magnetic toy train

Experiment 1

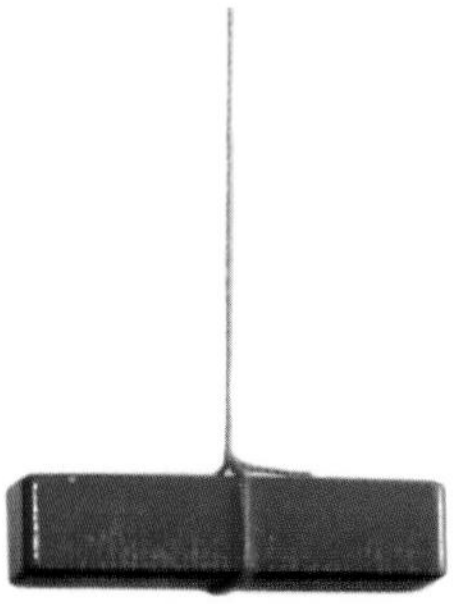

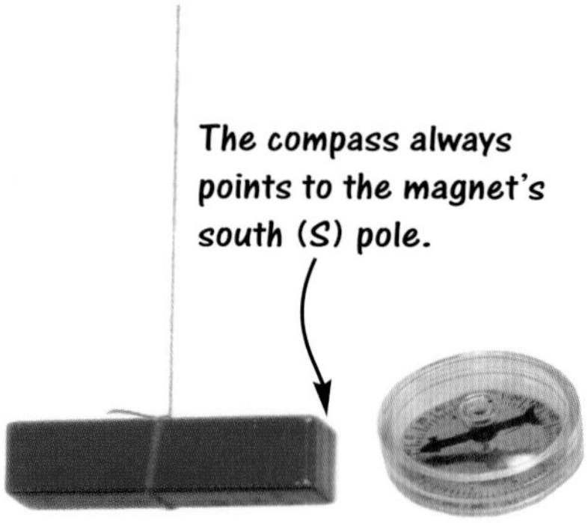

The compass always points to the magnet's south (S) pole.

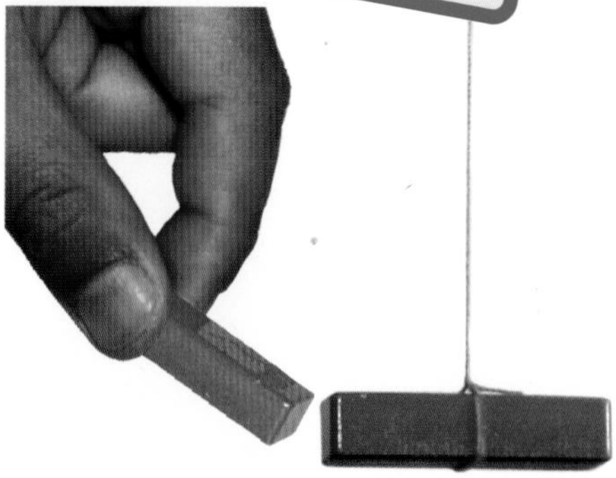

1 Suspend a bar magnet on a thread. Wait for it to stop moving.

2 If your magnet doesn't have 'N' and 'S' marked on it, use your small compass to find out which end is which.

3 Hold another magnet and bring it gently towards one end of the first magnet.

4 The hanging magnet will either *attract* or *repel* the other magnet.

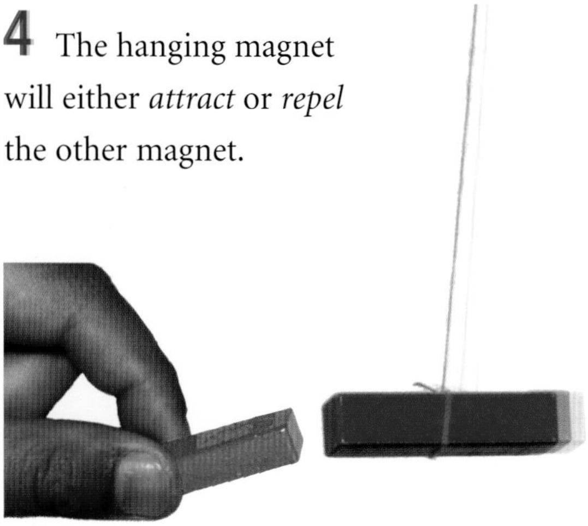

5 Try all the ways of putting the magnets' ends together. There are four. You get results like these.

N + N = repel	**S + S = repel**
N + S = attract	**S + N = attract**

What's going on?

Unlike poles attract and like poles repel.

Experiment 2

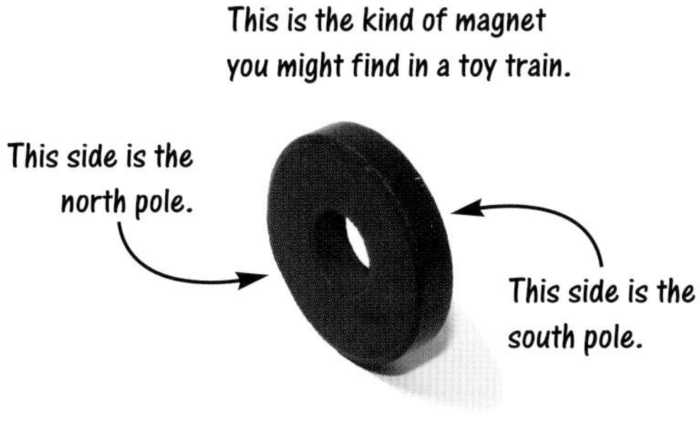

This is the kind of magnet you might find in a toy train.
This side is the north pole.
This side is the south pole.

1 If you have a young brother or sister they might have a toy train like this one with magnetic couplings. Can we explain why the train will stay together if the trucks are the right way round, and why it will come apart if they are not?

2 If you have a magnet with poles marked on it, you can test whether the magnets on the train have north poles or south poles facing out.

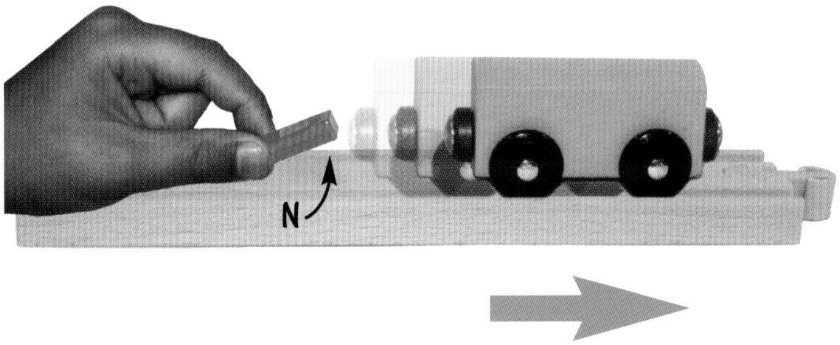

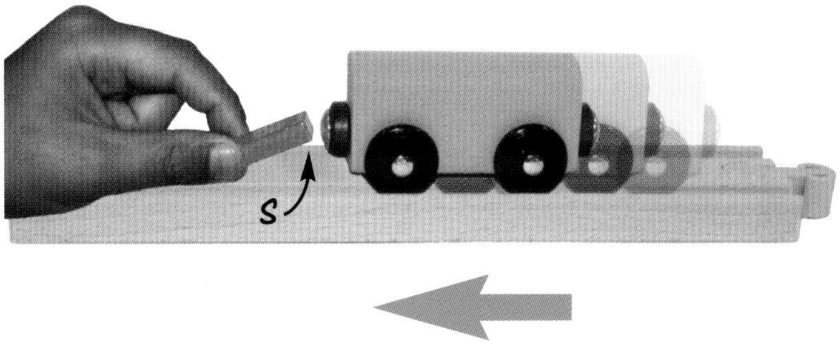

Knowing that like poles repel, this end of the truck must have the north pole of its magnet facing out.

Turn the magnet round, the truck will now come back along the track. Unlike poles attract.

What's going on?

If we know the *polarity* of one magnet, it can tell us the polarity of others. The pointer in a compass is a little magnet. The end that points to north is actually the north pole of the pointer.

Jargon Buster

Polarity means which way round a magnet is.

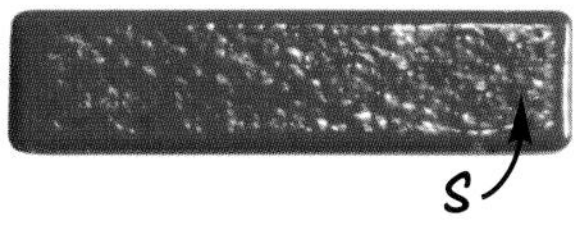

The magnetic Earth

35 minutes

A magnet has a north pole and a south pole and so does the Earth. What's the connection?

You will need:

- bar magnets
- a scrap of paper
- a small compass
- paper and pencil
- glass of water
- a needle, thread

The plan

We are going to experiment with some magnets and a simple compass.

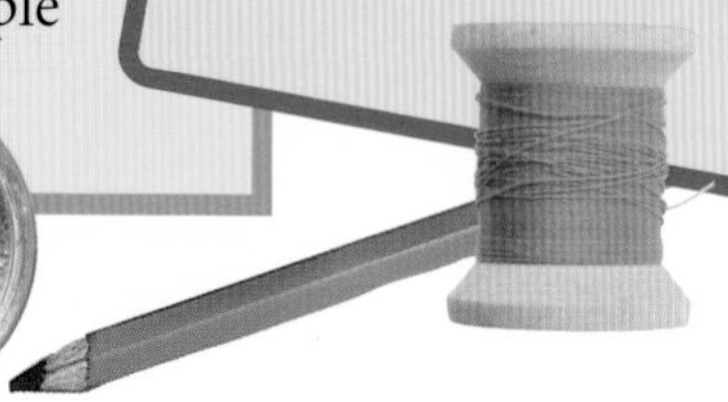

Experiment 1

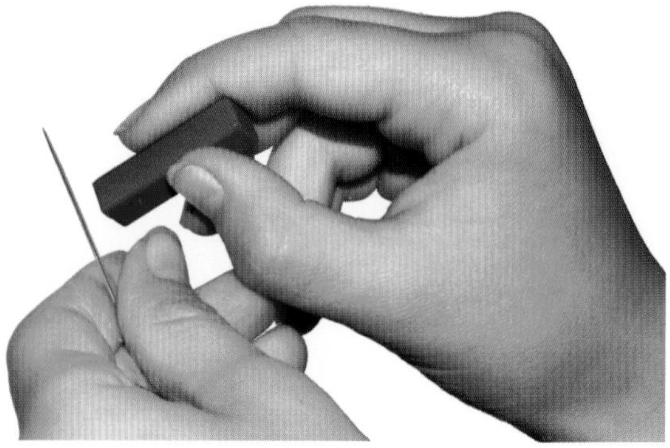

1 Magnetise a needle like the nail on page 23.

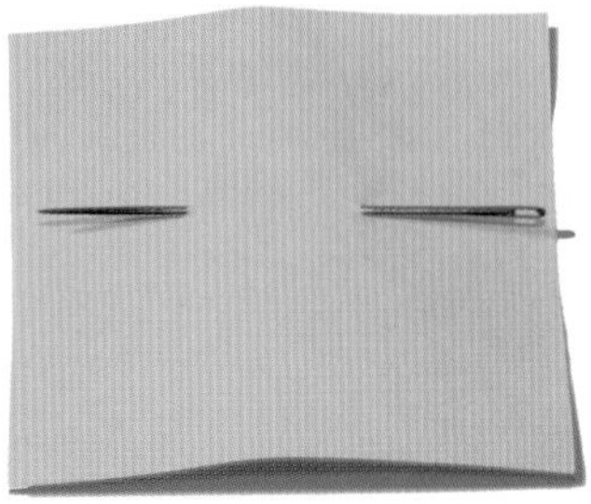

2 Thread it through some paper, like this.

3 Float it in a glass of water.

4 The needle will turn round until it settles, pointing north.

What's going on?

Inside the Earth there are massive amounts of iron. It's a huge magnet and our very small needle magnet is reacting with it.

Experiment 2

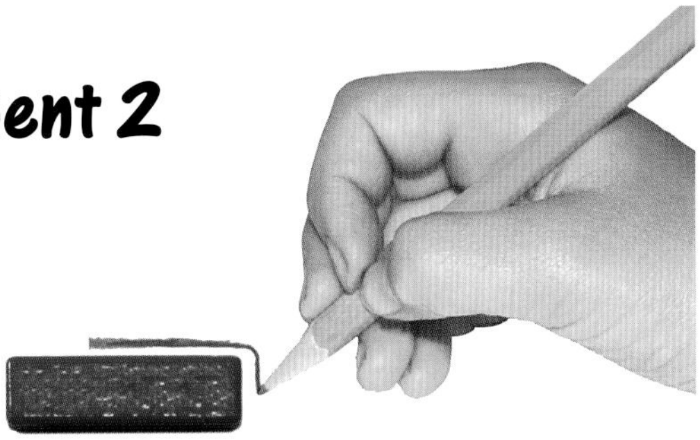

1 Put a magnet on some paper and draw round it so that you can replace it if it gets moved out of position.

2 Move a compass around the magnet in small steps. Draw arrows in each position to show the direction of the compass needle.

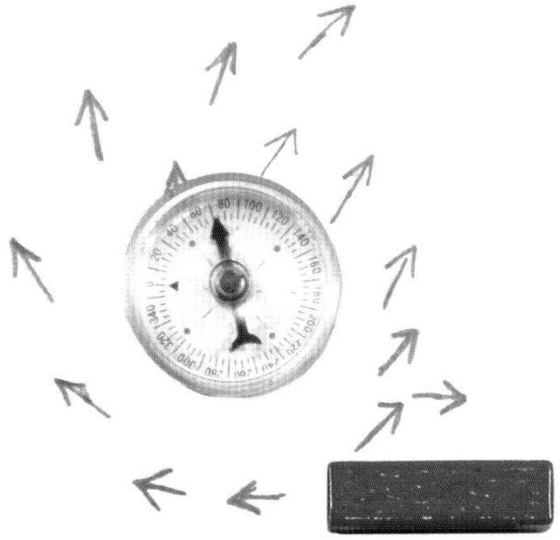

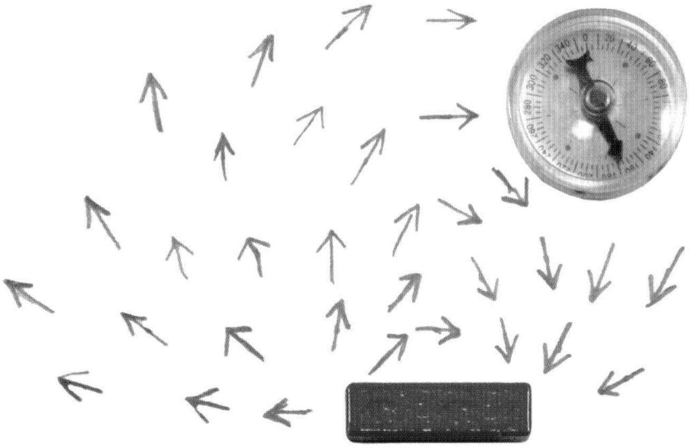

3 Continue drawing arrows all around the magnet.

4 The arrows are beginning to form a pattern.

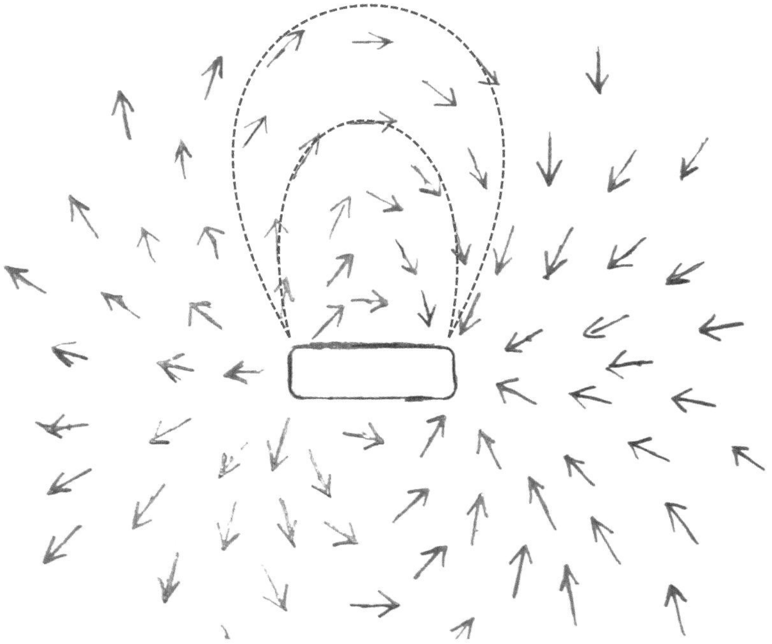

5 Join up the little arrows to make curved lines.

What's going on

You've drawn a map of a magnetic field! The magnetic field round the Earth is very similar.

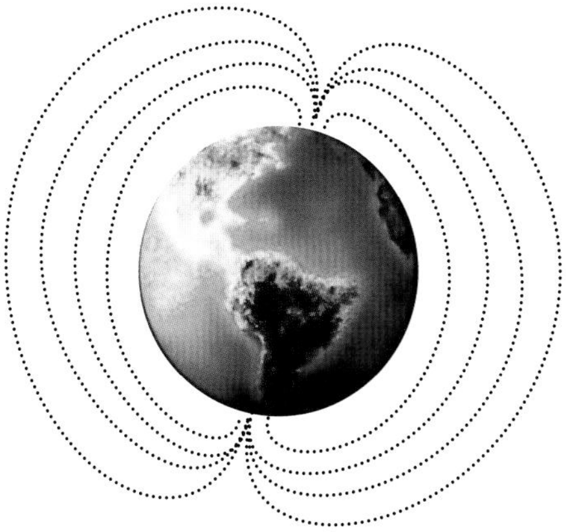

Electromagnets

Here are two experiments that show the connection between electricity and magnetism.

20 minutes

The plan

We're going to use electricity to make magnets.

You will need:

- circuit from Step 6, page 17 – with only one lamp
- about 600 mm (24 in) of insulated wire – the sort used in house wiring (see page 6) – with stripped ends
- large nail, sticky tape, pen, pencil, small compass

Experiment 1

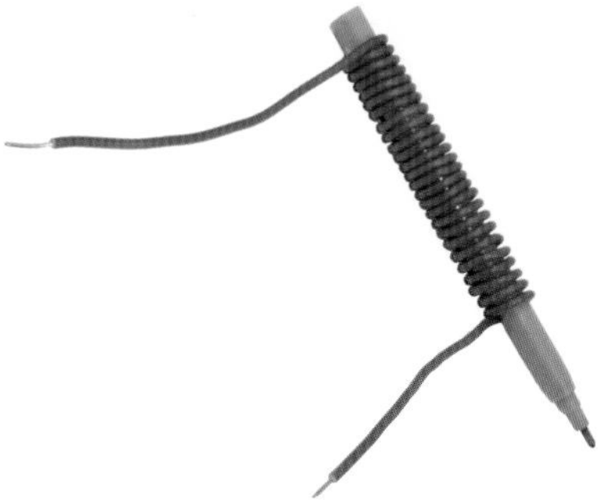

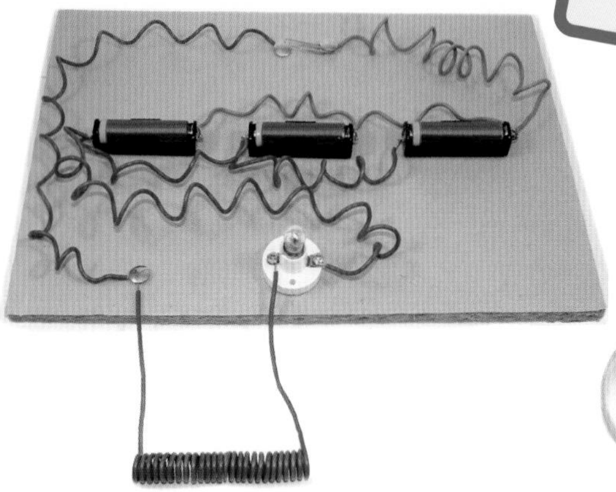

1 Wind the insulated wire tightly round the pen to make a coil.

2 Slide the pen out and connect the coil next to the lamp and switch on.

3 The lamp should come on, showing that current is flowing in the circuit. Test the coil with a magnet.

Experiment 2

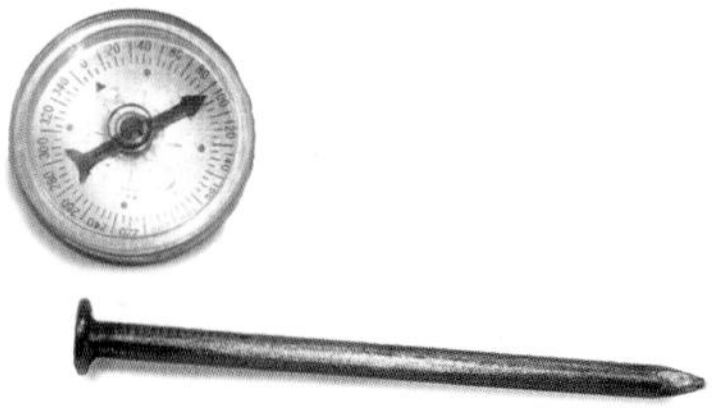

1 Make sure the nail isn't magnetic. Put it into the coil in the circuit as in Step 3 above. Switch on the current.

2 After 10 minutes, turn off the current, take the nail out of the coil and test with the compass.

What's going on?

In Experiment 1, electricity flowing through the wire has a tiny magnetic field round it. When the wire is coiled, the effect is concentrated and produces a magnetic field.

In Experiment 2, the magnetic field magnetises the nail.

Glossary

Attract To pull closer.

Bar magnet A type of straight magnet, with north and south poles at the ends.

Battery A store of electrical energy with negative and positive terminals.

Buzzer An audio signalling device, usually electronic, typically used in cars or in the home, for instance, in microwave ovens.

Circuit An electrical circuit is a network that has a closed loop, giving a return path for the current.

Compass A instrument for finding directions on the Earth. It consists of a magnetised pointer which always points north.

Conductor In science, a conductor is a material with low resistance, which means electricity can travel through it easily.

Insulator A material that resists or prevents the flow of electric current, for example, rubber.

In series If two or more circuit components are connected end to end like a daisy chain, it is said they are connected in series.

In parallel If two or more circuit components are connected like the rungs of a ladder, it is said they are connected in parallel.

Iron filings Iron filings are very small pieces of iron that look like a dark powder. They are sometimes used in magnetism demonstrations to show a magnetic field.

LCD Means liquid crystal display, a way of displaying shapes, numbers or letters by applying a current to liquid crystals.

Magnet A material or object that produces a magnetic field.

Magnetism A way that a material attracts or repulses another material.

MES Stands for miniature Edison screw and relates to a light bulb fitting. It is named after Thomas Edison, the inventor.

Molecules The smallest units of a compound formed by atoms bonded together.

Poles The ends of a magnet, north and south, where the magnetic forces are strongest.

Polarity Electricity and magnets have polarity. It's the direction that current flows in a circuit, or which way round a magnet is.

Repel To push away.

Index

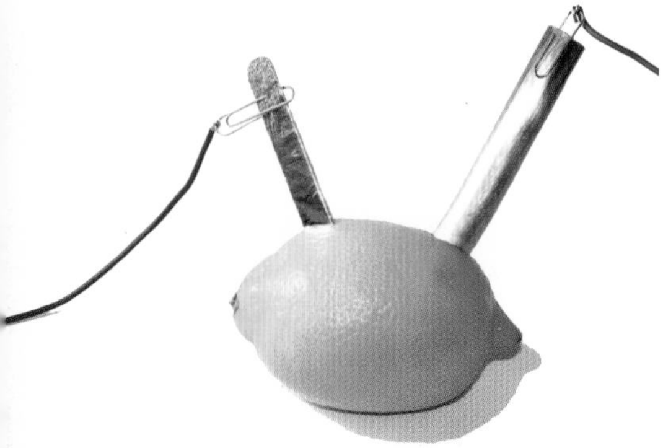

Websites

http://kids-science-experiments.com/
http://pbskids.org/zoom/activities/sci/
http://sciencemadesimple.com/
http://wow.osu.edu/experiments.php